What People ...

DEAR JOAN CHITTISTER

An epistolary tour de force, *Dear Joan Chittister* offers wisdom, grace, encouragement, gravitas, and hope. An inestimable gift for any reader, but especially young women of faith, persistence, desire, and authenticity.

» **KERRY ALYS ROBINSON**, *global ambassador of Leadership Roundtable and the author of* Imagining Abundance: Fundraising, Philanthropy and a Spiritual Call to Service

This little gem of a book is an easily accessible yet profound model of the kind of dialogue that is essential for an emerging generation of Catholic women to thrive in an institutional church that has forsaken them. With a pained clarity about their plight, yet an indomitable spirit of hope, these young women, who are so clearly called by God, are longing for the kind of wisdom and mentorship that Sr. Joan offers them in each warm, encouraging response.

» **JAMIE MANSON**, *columnist and editor at* National Catholic Reporter

In a time when more and more Catholic women are longing to speak honestly of the experience of womanhood within the church but are aware of the risks of doing so, this book comes as a force of intimate sisterhood to steady all our shaking knees and cracking voices—readying us for a more authentic, emboldened spiritual life.

» **SHANNON KAY EVANS**, *author of* Embracing Weakness: The Unlikely Secret to Changing the World

Down through the ages women mentors have sensitively guided companions in the sisterhood who seek to deepen their life in Christ. This tradition continues as Joan Chittister, OSB, wisely responds to women who desire to live fully and authentically in the church and in the world.

» **MICHAELA HEDICAN, OSB**, *Oblate Director and former prioress of Saint Benedict's Monastery in St. Joseph, Minnesota*

Breathtaking, hopeful, and sacred are my words to describe this collection. The exchanges speak to the human condition of being outside, being among, and refusing to be excluded. It's a blessing to be invited into the intimacy of their holy conversation.

» **ALISON M. BENDERS**, *Interim Dean of the Jesuit School of Theology of Santa Clara University*

The story of the American church today is not only one of silence and complicity. As this beautiful exchange of letters between Sr. Joan Chittister, OSB, and ten millennial Catholic women ministers reminds us, there is prophecy in sisterhood—still a place for speaking truths and hope for a church made new.

» **WILLIAM O'NEILL, SJ**, *Professor Emeritus of the Jesuit School of Theology of Santa Clara University*

Willing to name and wrestle with the challenges of womanhood, finding community, being Catholic, friendship, vocation, patriarchy, and questions of spirituality, these thoughtful exchanges offer wise counsel and sound companionship for other seekers of fresh truths.

» **GINA HENS-PIAZZA**, *Professor of Biblical Studies at the Jesuit School of Theology of Santa Clara University and 2019-2020 president of the Catholic Biblical Association of America*

Use these letters for your daily devotions, a small-group discussion, or a parish-wide conversation to discern your questions for a wise elder.

» **KATHLEEN A. CAHALAN**, *Professor of Practical Theology at Saint John's Graduate School of Theology and Seminary and director of the Collegeville Institute Seminars*

Over the last decades, many Catholics have wrestled with difficult questions about themselves and their church. But, often, at least in public, these questions remain unasked and unanswered. This book dares to hold these challenges up to the light of the gospel and search honestly for Christ.

» **JAKOB KARL RINDERKNECHT**, *Director of the Pastoral Institute at the University of the Incarnate Word in San Antonio, TX*

These millennial women are the beating heart of the Catholic church. This beautifully written and refreshingly honest book will ignite hearts, inspire action, and change the church. Every Catholic should read this book.

» **LUKE HANSEN, SJ**, *published writer in* America *magazine and* National Catholic Reporter

A much-needed dose of good news for our times, this soulful cross-generational conversation of women committed to life-sustaining friendships, authentic mentoring, and learning from the "sisterhood of saints" has left this reader in awe of what God is doing today through them for church and society.

» **EDUARDO C. FERNÁNDEZ, SJ**, *Professor of Practical Theology and Ministry at the Jesuit School of Theology of Santa Clara University*

To my pilgrim buddy Catherine,

DEAR JOAN CHITTISTER

Conversations with Women in the Church

JESSIE BAZAN, EDITOR

Cath,
#shabbat forlyfe.

TWENTY-THIRD PUBLICATIONS
twentythirdpublications.com

Dedication

To our wisdom figures,
conversation partners,
family, and friends:
thank you for your love
and encouragement.

TWENTY-THIRD PUBLICATIONS
One Montauk Avenue, Suite 200 • New London, CT 06320
(860) 437-3012 or (800) 321-0411 • www.twentythirdpublications.com

Cover photo: ©iStock.com / artisteer

ISBN: 978-1-62785-486-3 • Printed in the U.S.A.

 A division of Bayard, Inc.

CONTENTS

CONTRIBUTORS

JESSIE BAZAN earned a master of divinity degree from the Saint John's University School of Theology and Seminary and a bachelor of arts degree from Marquette University. She works for the Collegeville Institute on two ecumenical grant initiatives aimed at helping Christians discover and deepen their sense of God's calling in their lives. Bazan is also a columnist for *U.S. Catholic* magazine.

ELIZA BIDDLE is a high school teacher and educator from Wollongong, Australia. She has worked in Catholic education since 2013 and completed her masters of theology (Catholic education) in 2017. Biddle currently serves as the religious education coordinator at St. Joseph's Catholic High School, Albion Park, Australia, where she hopes to carry out God's work by creating meaningful learning experiences of the revealing power of Jesus' Good News for teenagers and young adults.

LISA CATHELYN currently serves as director of campus ministry at Alverno College in Milwaukee, Wisconsin, a Catholic women's college. Formed deeply in feminism and Ignatian spirituality, Cathelyn has experience in liturgical preparation and presiding, Scripture study, bilingual prison ministry, and significant international immersion experience, including a semester studying in El Salvador, teaching English in Vietnam, and contextual coursework in Israel-Palestine. Cathelyn earned her honors bachelor of arts in Spanish from Marquette University and master of divinity from the Jesuit School of Theology in Berkeley, California.

JOAN CHITTISTER, OSB, is one of the country's key visionary voices and spiritual leaders. A Benedictine Sister of Erie, Pennsylvania, Sister Joan is an international lecturer on behalf of peace, human rights, women's issues, justice, and contemporary culture. She is an award-winning author of more than forty books and hundreds of articles.

TERESA CODA has a masters in divinity from Harvard Divinity School and now works in parish ministry and hospital chaplaincy. She lives in Providence, Rhode Island, with her husband and daughter.

ALLISON CONNELLY was born and raised in Knoxville, Tennessee, and graduated from Vanderbilt University with a bachelor of science in child studies. After graduating, she completed a year of service with the St. Joseph Worker Program and spent several subsequent years working at various nonprofits in Minneapolis, Minnesota. Currently in her second year of graduate studies at Union Theological Seminary, Connelly identifies as belonging to both the Catholic Church and the United Church of Christ and is planning to be ordained in the latter.

MEGHAN DANDREA has masters degrees in education, theology, and ministry. She has over ten years of teaching experience at the high school and collegiate level. Outside of the classroom, Meghan is an avid traveler, a passion she extends to her students through international mission work.

ELLEN JEWETT is a master of divinity student at the Jesuit School of Theology of Santa Clara University in Berkeley, California. She has worked in high school and college campus ministry as well as parish ministry. Her research interests include artistic expressions of faith practice and the interactions among gender, race, and spirituality.

VALERIE LUCKEY, OSB, is a scholastic in the Erie Benedictine community, having made her first monastic profession in October 2017. She currently ministers at the community's child development center, Saint Benedict Center, where she runs and plays with toddlers each day.

LIZ PALMER is a minister and advocate for women. Originally from Grand Blanc, Michigan, Palmer studied biology and psychology at Saint Mary's College for her undergraduate education and completed her master of divinity at Loyola University Chicago. She currently lives in South Bend, Indiana, and serves as a rector at the University of Notre Dame.

JACQUELINE SMALL is in initial formation with the Benedictine Sisters of Erie. She obtained a masters of divinity from Princeton Theological Seminary in 2016, and a masters of social work from Rutgers University in 2017.

INTRODUCTION

Dear Reader,

Halfway through the inaugural Joan Chittister Institute for Contemporary Spirituality (JCICS), ten millennial Catholic women crammed onto a raised platform for a panel discussion on hopes, struggles, and the future of the church. We traveled from across the country—and even Australia—to learn from Joan Chittister and connect with other women asking similar life questions. The two weeks we spent with the Benedictine Sisters of Erie ignited our hearts—and the publication of this book.

That night, our chairs formed a zigzag horseshoe as we scrunched to make space for all the panelists. After minutes of maneuvering, we were set—as long as no one needed to turn, lift, or bend anything. About thirty minutes in, amid a rousing dialogue on seminary life, the back legs of one of our chairs scooted off the platform. In a fluid motion, nine sets of hands reached for our middle panelist to stop her from tipping backwards. The audience gasped as she calmly reclaimed her balance—impressively, with almost a full beer still intact. Without missing a beat, another panelist grabbed the microphone and deadpanned, "Friend, thank you for demonstrating the experience of women in the church."

The community roared with laughter while the truth of her words sunk deep. Women and other marginalized persons know what it's like to be nudged aside—or not offered a seat in the first place. We know the edge can be a painful, lonely place.

If you find yourself there, please know: you are not alone.

The chair-tilt fiasco ended in smiles not stitches because other women reached out in support. This is church at its best—present, attentive, active. This is the church we experienced during our two weeks at the Joan Chittister Institute for Contemporary Spirituality. This is the church we invite you to be a part of through this book.

On the first day of the Institute, Joan mandated us to "speak our truths." As we grappled with our truths and found the courage to speak them to ourselves and then to each other, we began to dream of offering them to you. This book, *Dear Joan Chittister*, is a collection of our truths. We share experiences of sisterhood and living our truths in a world that would often rather have us be silent. We give these stories to you so that you might find the courage to speak your own truth wherever you please. We hope you can find or create supporting communities that hold your truths with reverence and awe.

The stories we share come from our personal experiences and are tied to a question or an insight for the great spiritual master, Sr. Joan Chittister, OSB. She responds to us with her prophetic wisdom at the beginning of each section and the end of each letter.

We hope our stories become the hands reaching out to pull you back onto the stage from the edge. As you read our truths, we hope that you are inspired to start conversations of your own:

- Who is part of your community?

- What truths do you long to speak?

- How might you stand up to the patriarchy and other injustices?

Thank you for your support,

Jessie

on
sisterhood

I sat in the huddle of a dozen people all analyz-
ing the present state of national affairs, all concerned about the negativity and mean-spirited tone that
now colors what was once called "The American Way."

Most of all, the social deterioration that went with the
culture wars worried everyone there. We were sitting at a
table where one generation, whose lives had developed in a
very different kind of society than is shaping younger generations now, judged the future of the country to be poor.
Very poor. Until, suddenly, the younger man to my left sat
forward in his chair, raised his shoulders, straightened his
back, and declared with full throat, "You're all forgetting
something," he said and paused thoughtfully. "The women
are coming. Just look at the numbers of women being elected
to positions everywhere—and women are not going to allow
this mess to go on."

Well, if the education statistics are correct, more women
than men are enrolling in college and going on for more
graduate degrees or professional certifications than ever
in history. If the rise in the number of women politicians is
correct, there is a clear presence of the women's agenda in
public decision-making arenas now. If social trends are correct, most women now engage in paid work as commonly

and for as long as their male counterparts. And, in addition, if self-reliance is still an American value, the younger generation is either marrying later or marrying less.

Indeed, sisterhood and the community of female support, understanding, organizations, and goals that have emerged in the process are now a phenomenon, barely one hundred fifty years old in the making. For a confluence of reasons—higher education, social change, urbanization, and systems—women, too, for the first time in history, also meet, talk, plan, and figure out their lives together. From the Women's Suffrage Movement to the Me Too moment, women have been searching out like-minded women to learn from, connecting with women leaders and encouraging one another to become a force in society. Independent of men. Distinct from men. Despite men everywhere—in politics, business, education, and even the churches. And they are affecting every level, dimension, and direction of society with them. More slowly than they would like, surely, but faster than any previous generation—physically separated from one another as well as the world—was ever able to do.

Younger women today take these things for granted. They have their eyes on positions and places of power. They want change but not just any change. They want development that honors their own experiences and aspirations. They want to live fully human, human lives. They want to get the woman-man balance right. They want to be seen as disciples of Jesus, called to do a mission—even in the church.

Then they are amazed to find out that the glass ceiling is still a ceiling, even for them. Less visible now, yes, but no less there.

The questions they are asking themselves as they go sound the knell: Tomorrow will no longer be a repetition of yesterday. They are bent on figuring it out for themselves. And so this dialogue about it...between me and them.

Joan

Dear Joan,

My mother gave me so many gifts: self-reliance, a reverence for libraries, nightly family dinners, an understanding that you must take action whenever your conscience aches. But she didn't give me a sister.

It never occurred to me to be troubled by that when I was a child, and she gave me no indication that she was troubled either. But one day, when I was about thirteen years old, she apologized to me for this void in my life.

"I was thinking," she said, remorse soaking each word, "my sister is the most important relationship I have—the person I've known the longest, who understands me and loves me without question. We were girls together, and we're women together. And I wish I had given you someone like that."

I was in the habit of rolling my eyes at most of what my mother said to me at that age, but I sensed that this mattered too much for adolescent hostility. We sat silently for a few minutes, thinking about this predicament I was in, thinking about what it meant.

Then she said, "Alright. Here's what you'll do. From now on, I want you to think of every woman and girl you meet as your sister. I don't want you to compare yourself to them or think of them as competition. You can just know that you're women together and try to love them, and let them love you."

I recognized, even then, that she had just described the person I wanted to be.

I've failed to fulfill her mandate countless times, but I do try to be a sister to the women and girls around me, even those who intimidate me or test the bounds of my patience. And being a sister among sisters has been its own reward. The young girls I mentor, the women I came of age alongside, and the wisdom figures who share life with me bring me joy and grief and rage and hope. And fullness, always fullness.

You, of course, know what this is like, after more than fifty years in a women's religious community. And your writings, from *Heart of Flesh* to *Friendship of Women*, prove it. You know that the intimacy and trust between sisters can bring us to sterile domestic violence shelters, ugly jail cells, and chilled hospital rooms, just as it can lead us to eye-watering laughing fits, hard-won graduation ceremonies, and searing honesty on late-night long-distance phone calls.

I wonder: how can we encourage more women to recognize each other as sisters? Women are so often pitted against each other and undermined. We're taught from childhood that there is no higher compliment than "you're not like other girls." It's difficult to break through that conditioning.

But we both know that this will be a different, better world when we refuse to feel superior to or threatened by other women and when we let them really love us, however flawed and powerful we may be. I hope that a greater sense of shared sisterhood is coming, in my own life and throughout our culture. And I hope you and your community, with all your experiences as Benedictine Sisters, will continue to show us how it's done.

Yours,
Jacqueline

DEAR JACKIE,

Your letter strikes a range of chords in me. I have been dealing with the subject of sisterhood, of womanhood, all my life.

Like you, I had no sister; I am an only child. When I grew up, that was considered a decided disadvantage. People were more likely to say, "Oh, you poor child," at the thought of my growing up alone than they were to say "how wonderful" it was that I was an independent girl-child.

Nor did any of them seem to realize or understand the implications of what it means to be a girl alone in society rather than a boy. Boys could play sports and so had built-in companions whether they had siblings or not. Boys could roam at will while girls' outside activities were limited, socially defined, monitored. Boys were encouraged to get jobs and so got the money that went with them. Girls got "allowances"—small ones—because "girls didn't need money as boys did." Boys went on camping trips, business trips, family trips with their fathers, their teachers, their boy scout leaders. In unending ways, boys were mentored into the male skills and the male responsibility they needed to take on the world.

Girls, on the other hand, were expected to stay at home to help their mothers, to continue the world as they knew it, to do the housekeeping women were meant to do. Any ideas about a future for women beyond that were largely ignored.

Most of all, girls—especially those without sisters to lean on—lacked the model of older, more experienced women. Mothers, of course, molded the lives of generations of daughters but were of little currency in the search for more experienced public insights or as editors of women's lives in general. We all knew they were going to marry one of these

world-changing boys rather than become a leading professional or self-sustaining adult themselves.

Still, however little social norms encouraged women's
groups or women's discussions as tools of development, I
discovered better. Women totally beyond the boundaries of
the family introduced me to the world and changed my life
forever. Without them, I wonder if I would be writing this
letter to you today.

The first woman who enabled me to think beyond the
mold, a swimming coach at the local YWCA, took my young
middle-school years and turned them into possibilities.
From her, I experienced the chance of being heard. I got a
vision of what it was to be an independent woman.

She was physically beautiful, long-legged, secure,
and entirely at ease with herself. Without saying a thing,
she taught me to want to be the same. She coached me
into a junior lifesaving certificate before I was thirteen.
She grew me into the ability to endure, to have confidence, to find the kind of inner strength that hours in a
swimming pool forms in a person. By the time I left those
YWCA years for high school, thanks to her womanhood, I
was intent on becoming a responsible, sturdy, self-directed
woman myself.

Then the greatest of all the womanly influences in my
life—real Sisterhood—took over. The Benedictine Sisters
of Erie, and, in many cases, women religious everywhere,
taught me the power of spiritual solidarity. These sisters,

without a man in sight, demonstrated spiritual purpose, the power of which I had never before seen.

I watched these women create public projects and accomplish them with few resources but the holy intention it took to complete them. They designed, built, and administered their own academy and paid for it themselves. They pooled their talents and encouraged the young women who came after them both to achieve academically and to succeed in the public arena as well.

The sisters made human community real. Strangers to one another when they came to the monastery, they became one another's keepers for all their lives. It seemed as if they had decided that their common heart was up to scaling any mountain in front of them as long as they were doing it together.

They were educated in every subject. Women religious, they were nevertheless professionals in a world where professional women were few and far between. They proved that a woman does not become less womanly as she grows into the fullness of her womanhood. On the contrary, they helped us move from childhood to young adulthood and supported one another, as well.

The sisters were women who valued women. They were strong personalities who set the sights of my generation on spiritual depth and on the wisdom figures of life; they were women who took their place in the modern world as women religious had for centuries, with the gospel in one hand and a list of human needs in the other.

They were women who imaged the community of women beyond any of the limiting definitions of women being sold to them by either state or church. They showed other women how to reach beyond the boundary lines of the male society and become who they were rather than who men said they were to be. They did not shrink from life, and they formed us to live it fully, as well. It is that modeling of women with and for women that creates real sisterhood. The image of the sisters changed me. They stretched me to think beyond myself as woman to the needs of women everywhere; they encouraged me to dream daring dreams and to pursue them. It was, in the end, sisterhood that brought me home to myself. May it forever do the same for you.

Most important of all, may you yourself enable women to join together for good, to support and encourage other women, to see womanhood as the missing dimension of a just and equal life in both church and state.

As your mother told you, Jackie, love every woman you meet in ways that help her become the fullness of herself. Then our sisterhood, too, will be both the gift and the beacon that it is meant to be.

With affection,
Joan

Dear Joan,

I remember going home from second grade one day, carrying a picture that I had drawn of St. Thérèse of Lisieux surrounded by flowers. As my teacher spoke with reverence of Thérèse's "little way," she pointed out in front of the whole class that I was named after this special saint. I could have bubbled over with pride!

My balloon deflated just a little when my mom met the school bus and corrected the assumption—I'm actually named after St. Teresa of Ávila—and it burst entirely when I asked to see a picture of St. Teresa. The image my mom found was a drawing, of course, and it bore none of the rosy vitality of Thérèse's photo. I was devastated and wailed, "I want to be named after the pretty St. Teresa!"

Oh, vanity of vanities!

Over two decades later, the disappointment of that afternoon is long gone, but the pride of the morning is not. It delights me to be named after St. Teresa of Ávila and to share a name with two other amazing women in our church history: St. Thérèse of Lisieux and St. Mother Teresa of Calcutta. I am in a sisterhood of Teresas and gain strength and wisdom from each of these women.

St. Teresa of Ávila, who used her gifts and the gifts of her female contemporaries to reform the church, reminds me that power is not reserved for those who have clear positions of power. Teresa of Ávila knew that God dwelled within her and that she had ideas, skills, and insights to share with the world, for the good of the world. She didn't let anyone silence her.

St. Thérèse of Lisieux, who may be known as "the little flower" but had a will of steel, reminds me that God is in all things: the tender touch of a caring friend and the gentle breeze of a spring day as well as the frustration of a challenging task and the grief of the loss of a loved one. There is no one and no thing that can separate us from God, Thérèse makes clear. Her insight equips me to live life with attentiveness and fearlessness.

St. Teresa of Calcutta, who heard and refused to ignore a surprising call from God, reminds me of the importance of persistence: in work, in my spiritual life, in my relationships. Mother Teresa persisted when she didn't know if her plans would succeed. She persisted when she was met with external opposition. And she even persisted when she questioned her reasons for persisting. Mother Teresa's example invites me to carry on in the face of adversity.

Joan, I am nourished and strengthened by the sisterhood of saints. I wonder, which saints have inspired and invigorated your spiritual journey? Who has helped you become the person you are?

Sincerely,
Teresa

DEAR TERESA,

Your letter about names and their meanings stirred something in me that I have never thought of before. You helped me to realize that identity—yours and mine and everyone else's—is made up, like stained glass windows in even the smallest of churches, of multiple images and their multiple meanings. Slivers of different colors and shapes go into the forming of our lives. My identity is not one thing: it is the result of many things. It comes out of what we believe about life, what we value in life, what we seek to do with our own lives.

Most of all, identity is a movable feast. It is not a fixed concept. It is an esoteric kind of reality that slips in and out of focus in us as life changes around us and, in this modern society, as we ourselves change with it. So its importance to our emotional, spiritual self is painfully clear. Identity grounds us, beckons us, and guides us on through the rugged undergrowth of life as well as to its mountaintops. The point is that we all go through life as much in search of our essential selves as we are in search of God. To become adult, to be happy, to be fulfilled, we need to ask and answer two fundamental questions: Who am I? And, what am I meant to do here?

Like you, I spent a lot of my young life making regular visits to church, trying to identify my place in the pantheon of saints. When the light streamed brightest through the colorful church windows and the great nave was empty, I walked up and down the aisles stretching my neck to study the glass figures, trying to discover what the pictures had to say to me about my own journey on earth. I looked always and forever for women saints, of course. They were painfully few. St. Martin, yes. St. George, of course. Sts. Peter and Paul and twelve Apostles were everywhere there for the boys. None of them fit the identity I felt growing within me. The few small windows of women saints that were there, though no one talked about them, were important to me. After all, if even only a few women were there, were given places of honor in those windows—well known or not—it had to be possible for me to be there too.

The truth is that it's important to know who our heroes are and what it is that binds us to them if we ourselves are to form a strong sense of self.

Social psychologists tell us that the development of distinct identities carries us through life. Without models to steer by, Cote and Levine discovered, we may never become the fullness of ourselves. Instead, we stand to become unsettled and only partially developed adults. As a result, we may refuse to enter adulthood at all and become dependent on others. We can begin to drift through life, settling down nowhere and doing nothing of lasting value for anyone. As perpetual searchers, we go through life perpetually dissatisfied. Or, on the other hand, we may so internalize the past that we are incapable of change in a continually changing world.

But you, it is clear, identify with Thérèse of Lisieux, Teresa of Ávila, and Mother Teresa of India, strong women of great character. You plot them as models for yourself of persistence, spiritual power, and fearlessness, which, incidentally, is precisely the reason the church at one time mandated that the names of saints were to be part of the baptismal rite. Then, forever reminded of the great heroes of the faith who have gone before us, the child had a personal standard to steer by. It would, in other words, become part of their identity.

My list of holy s/heroes at this stage of life is too long to recount. They are everywhere. Nevertheless, Joan of Arc and Teresa of Ávila emerged in me somewhere along the way in my early childhood and hold privileged place in my heart to this day.

My one hope is that other women of your generation will find the women s/heroes who carry all of you to the peak of your spiritual development—for your sake and for the sake of a woman-denying church as well.

With affection,
Joan

Dear Joan,

Phoebe and I first met our freshman year of college at our school's Catholic center. We went through all of college together—the ups and downs, study abroad, roommate drama, long nights writing our respective theses, and even longer nights discussing theology and the role of women in the church. We laughed together (a lot), cried together, and, on at least one occasion, baked and ate an excessive number of cookies instead of doing our homework. We were inseparable. We were church to one another.

Our senior year, we both decided to apply to faith-based volunteer programs—Phoebe in teaching and me in campus ministry. I got my placement first, at a high school in San Francisco. For a few glorious weeks, we lapsed into fantasy. What if she was placed in Oakland? We could spend our weekends together, visiting the other's community, discovering the Bay Area, and finding a parish we could join. We could support each other as we both experienced life as working professionals for the first time. We could be home for each other. The lure of continuing our bond in such a way was intoxicating.

Then reality hit. Phoebe was assigned to a high school in Tampa Bay—2,908 miles away and three time zones ahead. We could only call each other occasionally on weekends, when we didn't have community activities and weren't exhausted from the school week. These phone calls were often difficult. Our stories involved people the other had never met. Our words often failed to convey our emotions, and, particularly trying, we couldn't give each other a hug when it was needed. Despite these obstacles, our friendship remains deep and life-giving. Phoebe and I still turn to each other both in moments of pain and in moments of joy, just as we did in college.

You write in *Called to Question*, "My friend is the one I see to be wiser than I. This kind of friend stands by in the midst of the spiritual whirlwind and holds out a hand on the rocks. [...] This friend simply frees us to be ourselves." Phoebe and I do just this for each other. We invite each other to grow into our true selves and explore our God-given callings.

Stability, both physical and relational, is a dream for many young people today, much like the shared San Francisco–Oakland fantasy. We move every few years for work and for school, struggling to maintain the bonds of sisterhood miles apart. Though Phoebe and I wish to live closer together, we have found a mode of stability in our friendship that transcends physical space.

So much of my faith life is derived from those around me and those with whom I share it. How do we maintain our close and essential female friendships through distance—both emotional and physical? Phoebe and I have managed, but it has been complicated. Long distance is never easy.

With love,
Ellen

DEAR ELLEN,

Your letter touches one of this present world's most poignant, most troublesome realities. At one level, "community" has come to mean a kind of contemporary nirvana, the stable place that knows and understands me, the place or person that becomes "home" for me in the midst of the angst in which I'm living.

At another level, community, the kind that generations before you once lived in and still remember, has disappeared. What's more, as we move from place to place and spend different parts of our lives with different people in different situations, this experience of revolving-door communities takes our school memories, our family traditions, and our best-friends-forever with it.

Yet, as you put it so well, Ellen, "community"—a sense of shared humanity, profound tradition, and common values—is as essential to our faith lives as it is to our emotional development and support. So what can we do to staunch this hemorrhage of human bonding? After all, being in a crowd is not the same as being in a community; crowds may even be, at best, an attempt to forget that we do not at present have a community.

No, the fact is that the answer to being part of something like "community" when distance divides us and personal amity is missing is as involved as the question itself. Military families, global institutions, and international marriages have all been dealing with this new global reality for years. And so must we.

The cost of such physical separation is clear: Immediacy, which is an integral part of being "best friends," of course, is diminished if not entirely lost. Planning, plotting, and the pursuit of common causes suffer from the strain of it. The awareness is keen that in case of emergency, or even any great joy—personal or professional—there is only the slightest chance that the one you would most like to share that time with will possibly be there to do it. The whole notion that your best friend is the one you can call at 3:00 in the morning and hear the words, "Stay right where you are. I'm on my way," is highly unlikely.

Nevertheless, there are gains too. Your relationship really depends now on communication of a more meaningful kind than physical presence. Talk time and confidences become more precious, more honest, more important than ever. In this case, you swap understanding for excitement or experience.

Finally, you yourself must become a builder of community. You must reach out and draw other people together. You will need to go to the places you most like—photography courses, maybe; local choirs, perhaps; volunteer programs, surely—because you know that other people who already share your interests are there waiting to solve both their loneliness and yours.

Finally, the irony is that it is the church itself, universal in nature, embedded in every culture, language, and politics, that has taught us the essentials of finding community in dry land. "Everywhere the church is the same," we were taught as children. "You will feel at home there." Point: It is in following our values that we find the friends with whom we can build new community, new holy friendship, wherever we are.

With affection,

Joan

Dear Joan,

In August 2015, I moved from Tennessee to Minnesota to begin a service year program with the Sisters of St. Joseph of Carondelet. The program, known as the St. Joseph Worker program, was built on the pillars of spirituality, leadership, justice, and intentional community with simplicity. Throughout the ten months of the program, the eleven other St. Joseph Workers and I engaged deeply with each pillar in a variety of ways, including participating in full-time internships with local nonprofits, one-to-one meetings with community leaders, political advocacy events, and quarterly retreats. However, out of all the carefully cultivated programmatic elements, the pillar that stuck with me the most was my experience of community.

Every Monday night, the four other women in my house and I gathered on the couches in our living room, bodies filled from a communal meal, and participated in the ritual we called Sharing of the Heart. We opened with sacred words, took time for individual reflection, and shared our present truths with the community: Where did you see God this week? What challenged you? Who are you thankful for? It was all held in trust by the group. Sharing our hearts with our community established intimate relationships.

In February 2017, about six months after ending my time in the St. Joseph Worker program, I came out as a gay woman. My community members from the St. Joseph Worker program were some of the first people I told about my sexuality. I received only welcome, support, and enthusiasm from my community. I basked in ways they celebrated me as I began to share myself more authentically with the world. These friends asked enthusiastically for details of my understanding of my sexuality, responding to my coming out with eager questions and excitement as they would to any of our friends beginning a new relationship.

Unfortunately, not all of my communities were as welcoming. Coming out as a Catholic woman, while beautiful and important, was also painful. I experienced rejection from old friends, previous sisterhoods, who used to count as community. When I shared with them my heart, my present truth, the ways I saw God in the fullness of my sexuality, my wonderings and my thanks, I expected to be held in trust by the group in the same way I had been held in my year of service. Instead, my trust was betrayed, my truth was discounted, my understanding of God was denied. One friend told me that my love was disordered and not what God intended for me. Another told me that she was glad I would never be able to get married in a Catholic church. And my rejection came, not only from people I had loved, but from a church I had loved, with whom I had also shared my heart.

Joan, I have had sacramental sisterhoods and sisterhoods that stop. As Catholic women we are asked, in prayer and ritual, to share our hearts with a church that so often does not hold us in the trust we deserve. Without sisterhoods like the one I experienced in the St. Joseph Worker program we cannot sustain our own participation in an environment as conditionally supportive as the institutional Catholic Church. How do we find truly "eucharistic sisterhoods" in ministry and daily life? Who accepts us for the full person we are?

Love,
Allison

Dear Allison,

Your letter breaks open in matchless and most poignant ways the very thing I alluded to in my letter to Ellen. The only difference is that you do it around a very sensitive and beautiful subject: the power of acceptance to release us from dejection by those who claim to love us unconditionally, as Jesus does. Unconditionally—whoever and whatever we are.

In the first program you describe, you experienced real community, the place where you could share yourself—your most personal struggles, your most foundational questions—because you were with those who accepted you and your questions with open hearts. In fact, you thrived because of it. You grew in authenticity and self-confidence. You were free to express and explore your most secret thoughts and feelings. So you trusted the honest questions, the genuine concern, the tender support of others.

In the second situation, you found a group that was pretending to be a community. In this place, the people who claimed to be listening literally could not hear anything but their own thoughts. Their hearts ruled out anyone whose experiences and understandings of life were unlike their own. They lived behind a wall of closed-mindedness.

For them, life is threatened by the very thought of difference even when someone else's difference does not actually threaten them at all.

Saddest of all is the fact that they believe that being church demands being closed to those who are different than they are. That to be judgmental is holy. That shunning is sanctifying. That condemnation of others is what their own redemption is about.

They forget that being gay is a very personal thing, an internal thing. It is a core component of the sense of self. The recognition of gayness, straightness, transgenderism is part of coming to the fullness of life. It is the glorious, life-giving act of self-awareness. At this point, a person begins to embrace the wholeness of the identity they know to be part and parcel of who they are as a person and what they have been created to be.

Interestingly enough, it is a process everyone must go through if they are truly to come home to themselves. However, in this case, Allison, this specific identity, yours, is now becoming universally recognized but not yet universally accepted or even understood. There are, then, Allison, some essential things for a person in your situation to understand.

First, do not be fooled: Courage has consequences. There are indeed some people out there who will reject you and try to reform you and think they have done a good and moral thing. However, if you and yours and the real Christian community can stand strong about the nature and fullness of creation, the church itself will be redeemed. Jesus didn't receive his crucified companions into heaven as he hung on the cross except to make us all rethink what God, what creation, what personhood and love *are* really all about.

Second, don't confuse acceptance and understanding. Acceptance takes nothing but tolerance, and tolerance will never spawn Christian community. Understanding takes time and holiness.

Third, let authenticity be the sermon your life speaks. Then, and only then, can the rest of us become authentic ourselves.

With affection,
Joan

Dear Joan,

My woman wisdom figure and I met during a difficult season of life. Instead of enthusiasm on the brink of my third and final year of graduate coursework, I felt weariness and exhaustion from the challenges of existing as a lay woman in a male- and clerical-dominated seminary. These fueled doubts about my own abilities and questions about future job prospects.

I attended a retreat in early September and found myself in a small group with a striking, red-haired, tall woman. She was ethereal and definitely had a mystic vibe. Lo and behold, her name was Chris.

She changed my life.

The initial exchange was a profound moment of recognition. Chris received a thank-you note from a Jesuit ordination earlier that summer that included an anonymous photo of a woman on an altar. That woman was, well, me, sitting in front of her in the flesh. Tears welled up in our eyes. I felt so seen. The hallowed encounters continued on the retreat when we brought identical Scripture passages to share: Luke 7:35–50, the story of the woman who washed Jesus' feet with her tears.

Scarcely one month after meeting, I learned of Chris's seizure. She would be undergoing major brain surgery, and we did not know the prognosis. In the days leading up to her surgery, Chris spent a lot of time in prayer, sorting out if she was in right relationship with God and staring mortality in the eyes. One fruit of this prayer was a specific request for a liturgy. She summoned four women, including me, to offer a liturgy of healing in anticipation of her surgery. Chris's ability to gather a sisterhood of women across generations and experience was inspiring. Chris called forth our gifts, truly a grace of sisterhood.

As we anointed, blessed, shared the word, and had communion, Christ brought a new form of sisterhood to the forefront—one of empowerment. On the eve of a surgery for which none knew the outcome, Chris boldly called forth our gifts and ensured each of us would have this mantra inscribed in our hearts: the people of God are in need of my gifts.

I am happy to report that the surgery went beautifully. As Chris adjusts to a new normal with a brain injury in San Francisco, and I delve into full-time college ministry in the Midwest, she still reminds me of my inner light and authority.

Sisters can see you in all your glorious potential, encouraging and supporting you in all seasons of life. My friendship with Chris over the past year has taught me that sisterhood must span generations and unfolds through email exchanges, handwritten cards, poetry, and prayer.

Who are the sisters that support you? What gifts did others recognize in you in young adulthood?

With love and solidarity,
Lisa

Dear Lisa,

Your letter touches an area we seldom discuss. As we sit and wait for the church to grow beyond its arthritic and, at the same time, adolescent patriarchal control of the world, we give it entirely too much power over our development. The fact is that the church not only does not empower us but, at base, cannot empower us. In the final analysis, empowerment does not, cannot, come from public organizations. Empowerment comes, ultimately, only from within ourselves.

Empowerment actually depends on the way we define

who and what we are. It depends on what we ourselves identify as our gifts and what we determine we are meant to do with them. It depends on our willingness to become the rest of ourselves regardless of what the world around us says we are allowed to be.

For centuries they said that women could not be educated, could not be doctors, could not study within the hallowed halls of male universities, could not own property or take out loans. Could not do anything that males, the other half of the human race, took for granted.

Yet, strong women—women like Harriet Taylor, Mary Wollstonecraft, Jane Austin, Emily Bronte, Mother Jones—female humans all—began like Jacques DuBosc in the seventeenth century to make a distinction between "education" and "instruction." "Education" he defined as development of the whole person, arguing that women were as rational as men and just as capable of receiving intellectual formation and making creative contributions to society. "Instruction," on the other hand, was at best a list of canons or social rules designed to control women—their intelligence, their humanity, and their soul.

"Instruction," of course, the male university system could refuse to give a woman. After all, men owned and controlled the boundaries of the instructional system. "Education," the deep, personal development of their own interests and gifts, women found aplenty for themselves outside the institutions of the period.

Gutenberg and his printing press let the cat out of the bag. What had been available to men only, and then only to a few of them, became standard. Tutoring was a commonplace social exercise and, if the family agreed, as open to girls as to boys. Male and female teams of scientists, philosophers, writers became a model for other men and women thinkers. Finally, many women quietly began to read themselves into an education and enter the salons of Europe. Many started to write themselves. Their novels, essays, and poetry seeded the world around them with a very different image of the capabilities and possibilities inherent in women.

So, yes, the church can bar the door of ordained discipleship to women. Nothing proves who owns the church more clearly than that. At the same time, women must refuse to be refused the essence and practice of what it means to be a human being who is morally, spiritually, intellectually, and psychologically whole.

About fifty years ago, I argued that it was the task of my generation to heap up on the steps of every cathedral all the inherent sexism that was contained in the historical research, theological contradictions, scriptural interpretations, and spurious scientific understandings of women that had been cemented in our tradition. I argued that the normative male patriarchy had to be both confronted and contested or change could never come. We did that. Now this generation must make women's theological teaching, scriptural interpretation, homiletics, spiritual guidance, and liturgical presence an equally valued part of the dailiness of life.

Like your friend Chris, it's up to you to call women together, Lisa, to lead them to plumb the spiritual meaning of the gospel for themselves, to minister spiritually to the world by defining the difference between the Jesus who invited women to follow him and the church that denies it.

Only in that way can the next generation of girls and women see themselves *as part of*, rather than *outside of*, the central mysteries of the faith. That will be empowering.

In hope,
Joan

Dear Joan,

It had been a tough week. The weather alternated between thick, soggy heat and monsoon-type rain, neither of which were conducive to the service work we had planned, or my curly hair. Our original lodging was unexpectedly unavailable, so we took up residence in an active preschool whose plumbing was infested with cockroaches. Every trip to use the bathroom facilities was like going on an insect safari. We—OK, I—were tired, hot, hungry, and ready for the comforts of our first-world lives. Yet here we were, stranded on the side of the road in the middle of the Dominican Republic. We were precariously close to missing our flight. I sulked my way off the debilitated bus, marooned in my own misery. But then I heard laughter. It rose above the heavy heat and cut through the catastrophe of the present moment. Laughter. My students were laughing, and not just nervous uncomfortable chuckling but a bend-you-in-half-ache-in-your-ribs belly laughing.

Joan, as a Benedictine Sister, community is the foundation of your life and your writing. In *Wisdom Distilled from the Daily*, you explain that community, especially the kind envisioned in the Rule of Benedict, is not a reprieve from the concerns of the world but rather a model for dealing with its problems. Community, real community, is born from a shared common vision where concern for the other and for all replaces the strictures of individualism and self-advancement. In these real communities each person becomes a miracle for the others, where gifts and talents of every member are used in the service of support and empowerment of the whole.

This is the lesson my students lived on the side of that desolate and hot road in the Dominican Republic. Their laughter breathed new life into my weariness. Amid the unfortunate realities that had befallen us, they joined together in joy, a testament to the bonds that had developed between them over the course of this trip, and a greater statement about our school community that raised and nurtured these girls. Their eruption of laughter on the side of the road is the same laughter that floats across the tile and wood floors of our almost one-hundred-year-old school building. It is a laughter that has buoyed my heart countless times before, a laughter that has reached into my stress and darkness and pulled me forward with the gentle reminder that hope is never out of reach. Within the relative safety of our community, the girls develop into miracles for each other, and for me, as we navigate and endure together the tumult of adolescence and human existence. At the core of who they are, who we are as a school, is the hope of sisterhood and the joy of community. A sisterhood that doesn't flee from difficulty but one that embraces each other and searches for goodness amid any storm.

My students help me to grow every day; they sanctify me and push me to become better and holier, even when I feel like I deserve it the least. As their laughter on the side of the road brought me out of my self-inflicted misery, I wonder what other miracles people have offered to me that I've ignored. How many times has laughter and joy been tuned out because the noise of chaos seemed louder? I am grateful for their laughter, a privileged invitation to be counted among their sisterhood even when that invitation takes me on a two-week service trip to the scorching soil of the Dominican Republic.

Love,
Meghan

Dear Meghan,

Without actually saying it, you raise an issue in this letter that is commonly overlooked, generally underestimated, and routinely rejected—to the peril of everyone involved.

You paint a picture of stressful circumstances, at least for Americans who are accustomed to good roads, sleek tour buses, secure travel, and multiple options. A situation like that, even without the added burden of the pressure of travel time, is enough to tax a person's patience to the limits. Even a good-natured group, let alone a frazzled chaperone, could well be expected to reach the point of frustration far off the American scale of what exactly constitutes good times and exciting experiences.

You're honest about it. You admit the discomfort of it all. You describe the need to adjust to things like cockroaches, drenching rain, adverse bathroom facilities, and bad sleeping conditions. Most of all, you—leader, spiritual model, educational guru—own your dis-ease.

Then, realizing that the high school girls with you, the ones you are responsible for in a situation like this, are laughing, you laugh too.

Is the letter about joy? Well, yes, I suppose. But at the same time, no, I'm sure. More likely, the underlying message is about the place of support in life. As in "Lord, to whom shall we go?" as Peter says in Scripture when Jesus asks him if he's had all he can take of life on the edge, pressure from the people, rejection from the authorities.

Support implies the awareness that even though things are not as good as we would like them at any given time, there is someone, somewhere, who will stay with us while we deal with it. There is someone who will at least not make things worse. Someone who will not add to the feeling of guilt that comes when what we did not plan for threatens to wreck all the impressive things we did plan and looked forward to doing.

Support, we learn as one disaster after another assails us, is the real elixir of life. Tornadoes, hurricanes, thousands of acres of fire, broken hopes, a sandstorm of unseen obstacles along the way do bend us, yes, but they do not break us as long as we do not have to face them all alone. No, support does not compensate for our shattered expectations. It does, however, sustain us through them. Support does enable us to go on when it appears at first that there is no way, no energy, no reason to go on at all.

It is that kind of support, Meghan—calm understanding, patient listening, emotional venting, rock-solid trust, genuine empathy, and yes, gales of laughter to break the tension—that takes us up one side of the mountain of life and back down again, still committed, still willing to struggle on, still alive with hope. It is that kind of support that real sisterhood brings to the solitary life.

You enabled it for those girls. You modeled it. There is no greater gift one woman can give another. Give it always.

With care,
Joan

on speaking
our truths

AUTHENTICITY IS ONE OF THE MOST DEMANDING THINGS IN LIFE TO ACHIEVE. Being what we look like, becoming what we seem to be, is the task of a lifetime—if it comes at all for women.

If truth were known, it would become clear that life is one great sponge. The fact is that as we develop, we absorb the truths of life that swirl around us from somewhere else.

The dictums of parents become the first law of the land. The culling of our teachers, our elders, our authority figures become the road map from childhood to adulthood. Our truth becomes the distillation of the experiences of others. Their conclusions about life, their hot or cold commitments to the institutions of the day, their truisms become the compasses of our own hearts.

Then, before you know it, we are adults—and with the exception of our few bursts of standard adolescent rebellion—still thinking and doing the same things. Constructed half out of love, half out of fear, these great Truths of Life are impermeable, unquestionable, infallible. We say what is acceptable. We become the town criers of our cultures. We repeat the solemn local givens of life, too often without the slightest indication that there might be other ways to look at things. We echo the inventions and fictions of the age with perfect confidence. We tell and retell "what everybody knows," until, of course, some of the certainties inscribed on our hearts from days long past begin to fail us.

My father, a hard-working man, impressed on me, for instance, that if the work I was doing collapsed, I could always "get a job sweeping streets, doing dishes, or digging ditches, if necessary." There would never, he said, be a reason for me to take "charity" from anyone. Moreover, I believed him and hung my dignity on my commitment to it. Until I realized that when the city got electric dishwashers, and street sweeping trucks, and heavy equipment, there were no more dishwashing, or street-sweeping, or ditch-digging jobs to be had. The notion of public "charity"—Medicaid, or social security or child care, perhaps—was now a hotly contested social issue. Half of my confusion then came from my father's teaching, the other half from my experience and reflection.

Adulthood is what happens when we have tested our childhood assumptions, edited them, and found the courage to speak a new truth honestly, respectfully, and prophetically. We learn that we can create a new truth, our truth, despite the number of those who still want us to preserve a dead and deadening past for them.

Women's truths, especially, have been silenced for centuries, their agendas ignored, their insights either mocked or muted. But no more. No more. "The women are coming" with an agenda in hand. It's called Truth, Authenticity, The Other Half of Theology, and The Gospel Vision of Jesus.

Joan

Dear Joan,

Sacraments help me make sense of the world—and I stumble upon thousands of them every day. The created world teems with signs of God's grace. From sanctuaries to state parks, natural elements like water, fire, oil, and wheat help ritualize the work of the Holy Spirit in the ordinary. I'm particularly drawn to big bodies of water, which remind me of my baptismal call. The connection felt especially strong the time I entered into a pre-Triduum foot washing with a gracious partner: Lake Sagatagan.

On Holy Thursday afternoon, I made my way along the tree-lined trail of a local arboretum. It smelled of early spring. Dead leaves crunched beneath my sandals as I stepped further away from the stressors of school and work. We were entering the most sacred days. I needed to ready my body and heart.

When I got to a cove nestled just south of the trail, I removed my shoes—the only way to stand on holy ground.

I hopped to a rock islanded just off the land. My bare soles landed on the warm, wet granite. Around me the lake shimmered like it had just been doused with the world's largest tub of glitter. I bent down and, guided by the water's waves, massaged the dirt away from my soles. We worked in tandem, the water and I. It gave of itself freely. I did the same.

Joan, you know well the call of the human family to steward the gifts of creation with great care. You dared us to "imagine a world where stewardship, the care of the earth, became a living, breathing, determining goal in every family, every company, every life we touch."

I wish everyone had the chance to wander into the woods, or wash their feet in a lake, or lounge in the shade of a big oak tree. Then, their senses might be open to some beautiful truths:

> **Creation cares for us.** I am in relationship with water, just like I'm in relationship with the neighbor who washed my feet in church a few hours later.

> **Creation sustains us.** It gifts us with food, drink, shelter, oxygen, light, beauty, and many other essentials we need to survive. I live because it lives too.

Creation reflects God—and deserves to be treated as such. God is light. The sun gives light. God is hope. Rain after drought gives hope. God is peace. A gentle breeze gives peace. We come to know God through the natural world. Similarly, an attack on the natural world is an attack on God.

In the spirit of the movements of the Triduum, I wonder: What would it look like for the global church to lament the suffering of creation? What human habits need to die to save the earth? How can we help the environment resurrect so that it can continue to be a life-giving home for generations to come?

Peace,
Jessie

DEAR JESSIE,

I paused at your letter differently than I had at the ones before it. It's a beautiful letter. It's the kind of letter I wish were being preached from every Christian pulpit everywhere. But it is not. For the first time in history, Pope Francis's encyclical *Laudato Si'* links our treatment of creation—animals, plants, resources, and people—with what it means to live a moral as well as a spiritual life.

Up until this point, only humans counted as necessary parts of the creation equation. All of creation, we taught—we crowed—was for our use. We could do whatever we wanted with it. However, a theology of creation like that has consequences:

First, we come to think of Creation as a procession of stages, each plane higher than the one before it. From this perspective, humanity outranks the universe in splendor. It is, therefore, moral, imperative—godly—to put our needs above the needs of other creatures. As a result, we have drained marshlands, cleared forests, and displaced animals everywhere to build our cement jungles to solely human dimensions. In the end, ironically, we have jeopardized what we ourselves most need.

Second, man, the male, the presumed top of the pyramid, is the crown of creation. Best of all, we know it's true because men told us so. In maleness is creation's peak, its only entirely rational creature—whatever that errant little phrase "let us create them in our own image" might also mean. Obviously, then, what women think or want or need is lesser, secondary, derivative—and certainly without priority. Instead, it is what men have said that women think or want or need that has become "a woman's place," "the law of the land," the "will of God" for them. Or to put it another way: Everything that was written about us was written without us.

Third, therefore, men are God's agents on earth. They own nature—and the women in it—who are not quite as human a human being as are males. It's men who are the agents of God on earth, they reason. It's men who control it, have it for their use—and all for nothing.

Knowing all of this, Jessie, your questions make sense and are determinative, both for nature and for women. Defined as less rational and closer to nature than men, women are then, to all intents and purposes, left out of the problem-solving equation of the human race.

For a global church to lament the suffering of creation, it would also have to grieve the conditions of women in the world—women whose life-giving part of the natural world requires us to see life and its multiple agendas differently than men do. The church would also have to look differently at the conditions of animals and their place as part of the entire ecosystem. As a church we would need to develop the spirituality of humility on which the Rule of Benedict is based if we ever hope to make Right Relationships the foundation of our lives.

The agenda you posit is a big one. Without it, the future will simply be more of the present, only worse. At the same time, the gift of creation is that there are people like you out there who know that human beings—men and women—are part of nature, not above it. Most of all, they know that their own development depends on what we do with all of it. Mohandas Gandhi long ago gave us the answer: Be the change you want to see in the world, he told his followers.

It's you, Jessie, and so many like you, who not only know the change but are already making it. You are the hope I seek.

With courage,
Joan

Dear Joan,

In your book *Following the Path*, you remind us that there are three pivotal discernment moments in our lives: at early adulthood, at the proverbial "mid-life crisis," and at the final stage of our lives when we slow down and look back on our journeys.

I remember sitting in the room with you as you led a retreat on this book, thinking to myself, "And, here I thought I could discern once, make the big decision, and be done forever."

At that point I was twenty-six years old and teaching fourth grade. I thought I could find the right school that fit my teaching style; settle in the city I love; and be content with my career and, subsequently, my life.

Oops.

Because here I sit, at age thirty, a member of your religious community, the Benedictine Sisters of Erie. How did that happen?

Discernment happened.

When I left that retreat at the monastery in Erie, I heard a word repeated that you had repeated many times during our weekend together: authenticity. The priest at my parish gave a homily on living authentically as a way of living in God's presence.

I still remember sitting in the rocking chair on the second floor of my house later that day, the homily lingering, and me thinking: "I have to enter the community. I want to be an Erie Benedictine."

Ursula Le Guin, an American novelist, once told a group of graduates: "When women speak truly, they speak subversively—they can't help it: If you're underneath, if you're kept down, you break out, you subvert. We are volcanoes. When we women offer our experience as our truth, as human truth, all the maps change. There are new mountains. That's what I want—to hear you erupting. You young Mount St. Helenses who don't know the power in you—I want to hear you."

To enter religious life in 2018, you have to erupt a bit. You have to speak an uncommon truth. As women, it is often even more difficult to speak that truth living in a society controlled by a male-dominated agenda for what women should be. But being with the Erie Benedictine community, surrounded by women who have been erupting for decades, I finally knew it would be safe to speak my truth, not the truth of what others wanted for me or of what I thought I wanted for myself.

I want to live authentically. My authentic call is to enter religious life during a time when entering is no longer a truth accepted or understood by many. For me entering religious life does not mean entering a convent, as many phrase it, or becoming a nun, as others might say. It means giving myself to a communal life where we seek God together. It means giving myself to ministries that uphold the poor. It means giving myself to a ministry of prayer that unites my life with the Source of All Life. I believe it is the way for me to live most authentically.

That retreat you gave, titled the same as your book, "Following Your Path," began the path of my first pivotal discernment. Your call to speak our truth, to live our lives authentically, provided the fodder for deep reflection on my true calling. And, even though more discernment certainly lies ahead, and indeed, every day as I now understand, I say "Thank you" for the ways that weekend led me to find joy in living my truth. May each one of us attempting to live authentic lives find wisdom figures who can guide us through our discernment, both on the daily and in the long term, with open ears and abundant love. I believe this is essential, to discern with those who have traveled farther than we have. Joan, how else will be able to become our authentic selves if we do not discern how God speaks in our lives?

Love,
Val

Dear Val,

I think you have identified something in this letter that has been lost to our culture for decades now. The whole idea of wisdom, of growing into understanding through meaningful experiences, has given way to technological updating. Immediately. Quickly. Thoughtlessly. Just hit the blinking button and wait for the answer to appear.

In this new society, we find ourselves skipping whole segments of life at a time. What before this era of universal computerization would have required our living through a procession of new technologies, new learnings, new frustrations, new awarenesses, or new learning situations and devices slowly, one at a time, is now compressed beyond thought. This era moves us overnight, without preparation, from electrical connections to Bluetooth or Thunderbird or touch bars, with quickstart guides—not manuals to study—while we leap from one new way of doing things into another. Without ever providing the possibility to even evaluate the one we just traded for another one.

We're told now that computerization is reconfiguring the human brain. Apparently, we think differently now. We come to conclusions differently now, the experts explain.

The problem is that while we speed up the algorithms of thought, the human heart still needs time for reflection, still needs calm and thoughtfulness, still needs space to evaluate the results, still needs wisdom—not velocity—to correct them. If we are to absorb not only the data we deal with but appreciate the value, the wisdom, of any of it, we must be able to reflect on life as well as merely react to it.

In this era, in other words, wisdom, soulful reflection, has given way to speed as we get accustomed to one new baseless possibility after another. This is a time when we do what is new, not necessarily because we know it to be best, but because "new" is the hallmark of success in a world without spiritual criteria. It's the latest things that count, not the wisdom to identify the most profound, the most meaningful, the most humane.

The spiritual problem of the day is that we hardly have time in such a society to be sure ourselves whether or not we are living the latest version of life or an "authentic" life, whatever version it may be. A life predicated on clear values, deep reflection, grand purpose, and honest and open awareness of the inner inclinations of the soul, of the self, is an authentic life. Anything else is, at best, a plastic copy of one.

Up until the end of WWII, it was common for extended families, two or three generations of one family, to live together or at least near to one another. Three and sometimes four generations went through all the circumstances of life, each in their own way, but in tandem. Which means that one generation learned from another. Discernment then was a matter of thinking through the multiple world views before us before choosing the one that had the most impact, that made the most sense to us and our own stage of understanding.

When you talk about "finding wisdom figures who can guide us through our discernment," you are talking about mining the insights of those who have gone before us and have come out the other side of life healthy, happy, and holy because of it.

You are talking about one of the primary reasons that Benedict of Nursia made the notion of community itself, not ministry, not asceticism, not even military obedience, the essence of life. Benedict knew that "community" is what grows us, what authenticates our holiness, what carries us through periods of the spiritual life we might otherwise abandon if not for the support and model of those who have gone before us.

Indeed, in a woman's community, in any community of serious seekers, we have that extra something of wisdom models all our lives. Then false holiness cannot vitiate the spiritual growth that emerges, even if cautiously, in the truly authentic life. It is life lived honestly, with itself, always striving for depth, forever growing beyond its inner child.

With support and community love,
Joan

Dear Joan,

In your book *Radical Spirit*, you write that the third step of humility, as outlined by Saint Benedict so many centuries ago, can be understood to mean that we must "seek direction from wisdom figures." You explain that we can't always make the right choices with our limited knowledge and experience, and I know that's true: the mentors I've had have offered me grace and insight through all kinds of early adulthood dilemmas. And the best direction I've received has come when those wise people weren't advising me at all—when they were simply letting me watch as they lived their lives, made their choices, and took their stands.

Take Sister Mary Lou, for example. At a political demonstration we both attended a few years ago, she did something that taught me more about courage and principles than any conversation could have done.

It seemed like half of Erie turned out for this demonstration: Benedictine Sisters, other faith leaders, students, parents with children, news crews, and even politicians. One of those politicians was a woman who had taken some controversial stances in her career, though I didn't know that at the time. All I knew was that the man behind us in the crowd loathed her and was outraged that she was there. He was calling her vile, sexist names and accusing her of shocking crimes, not really talking to anyone in particular, but making sure that no one could avoid hearing him.

Joan, I didn't know what to do. I wasn't exactly afraid to speak up—I've had good experiences confronting the petty examples of cruelty and prejudice that the average person encounters from time to time—but, without knowing any of the context, I felt that I didn't know quite how to speak to him. I wanted to make some kind of well-reasoned, intellectual argument to persuade him that if he couldn't respect the politician as a person, he could, at least, not use misogynistic terms to describe her. I was just stuck, mentally composing and recomposing my case, as he raged on and on, louder and louder.

Then I saw Mary Lou turn to him, her jaw tight. "Hey!" she said, not loud, but serious, "That's my friend you're talking about."

His face bloomed red, and he seemed to struggle to find his next words. But finally, he said, "I'm so sorry."

I don't think "shocked" is too strong a word to describe how I felt in that moment. Mary Lou had overturned all my assumptions about how best to challenge bigotry and hatred, by aligning herself, unapologetically and unpretentiously, with the person the man was criticizing. She showed me then that speaking up doesn't need to be an academic exercise, and it shouldn't be about dazzling your opponent into agreeing with your superior rhetoric or morals. In fact, speaking up may not be about you at all.

Sometimes speaking up can be a matter of reminding those in power that victims of injustice are human beings too and are part of your community, loved and worthy of love.

I know there is much more to learn, and I am so grateful that wise people like you and Mary Lou will continue to give direction with your lives.

Jacqueline

DEAR JACKIE,

There are two folk stories that long ago captured the heart and mind of both Mary Lou and me. We've used these stories often; we've talked about them a lot. I don't remember which one of us discovered them first—we are both wisdom watchers of the highest degree. However, I do know the stories and why we immerse ourselves in them with such concentration.

First, I have a friend who says that there are no new questions on earth—and no new answers either. There are, he said, just new situations in which to apply the message. Or as Willa Cather, in *O Pioneers* put it: "There are only two or three human stories and they keep repeating themselves as fiercely as if they had never happened before."

His point and hers is that the human being is a human being everywhere, in all situations, always. We all contend with anger, betrayal, fear, love, joy—whatever the human responses that we happen to be dealing with at any given time. In fact, I wrote an entire book about them called *Welcome to the Wisdom of the World* in which I examine contemporary situations—like stress—in the light of the wisdom stories of other cultures and religions.

In the situation you mention, two of those stories come to mind. In the first, the neighbors press a local seeker to explain why he travels so far and so often to see a monk whose reputation for sanctity and strength of soul is legend. "Do you go to learn his prayers?" one man asks. "No," the seeker answers. "Does he give you rituals to do?" the second man asks. "No, never," the seeker answers. "Do you go to ask spiritual questions?" a third man presses. "Not at all," the seeker says. "Then why do you go there?!" the men say, frustrated with the answers. "I go to watch the master tie his shoes," the seeker says.

As you discovered, Jackie, what we ourselves do in moments of stress and failure, of tension and confrontation, of confusion and pain speaks far more loudly than any mere argument can possibly ever do. The answers to life's problems are never "answers" that end all answers. Answers change from situation to situation. It's the attitudes we bring to the question that count. It is in the cultivation of those attitudes—calm, commitment, loyalty, compassion, identification with the world—that we ourselves grow and become a sign of growth to others.

The second story that has shaped so much of what Mary Lou and I both honor is equally demanding. "If you want to smell sweet," the Sufi teaches, "stay close to the seller of perfumes." If you want to grow in courage, walk with the courageous. If you want to learn compassion, follow those of strong heart who go on comforting the suffering with little hope of changing the system itself. If you want to understand justice, volunteer in a soup kitchen. There, the rest of the population, meaning the ones who cannot hold a job however many jobs you give them, the ones who are handicapped and homeless, who are hurting in spirit, body, and mind, will bring you to understand that justice does not mean "sameness"—same rules, same expectations—it means "justice"—a decent life—for all.

In other words, go where what you want to become is a living flame. Then, you yourself may become a spark that lights it in others as well. Most of all, always, always,

always—whatever your own convictions and ideals, values and hopes for the world—burn on.

With fire in mind,
Joan

Dear Joan,

"You're upsetting the order of things," "burdening the institution," and "distracting the real scholars," he accused. "Take some time off; read some books; it is not like you'll be any use in the classroom," he advised.

"We've never done this before. These things take time and we move slow," he offered reassuringly, covering the subtext of "you don't matter" with holy water-laced words.

"Why aren't you more grateful?" she consoled. "Didn't you want this attention? Weren't you kind of asking for it?"

"It couldn't have been that bad," he said, his collar gleaming like it was woven from strands of Jesus' halo. "You're still going to his church, right?"

"No, not him," they spit. "He's so wonderful." Their voices in unison sound like an angelic choir.

These phrases settled like a rock between my shoulder blades, piercing each breath with renewed pain. Every tenet of what I had proclaimed to be true in word and deed, I now held in suspicion. Where could I turn when the place that was the foundation of my life was the place causing the pain? Did God love me? Is God in the church? Do I belong in the church? Was there a place for me, a woman, in the kingdom of God? Was there even a God to begin with?

I desperately wanted to shout my pain, to speak it until I couldn't breathe, to cough up all those words and to spit out the acrid left-over feelings of doubt and uncertainty. But he was an important and holy man of God.

I learned to swallow my pain and hurt, speaking the truth only to the statues of the saints that lined the walls of the church, their stony countenance silenced any objection to the story I poured out to them. A solitary ray nuzzled the marble feet of Jesus protruding from the base of the ninth station. Transfixed by the realness of his feet, I stopped to study the life-like and life-sized statue of Jesus writhing in the dust of his third fall. His mouth was pulled into a grimace, but his eyes remained focused forward. I followed his gaze down the walls of the basilica, the five remaining stations nestled into the wall lead to the glorious altar carved in red marble. It seemed like Jesus was contemplating what lay ahead of him, deciding whether to endure the torment yet to happen or to give up in the dust and sand of his third fall.

My fingertips traced the bones of Jesus' feet, and for a second I recognized in Jesus and in myself what you herald as the greatest virtue: endurance. The patient sustaining of Jesus in the midst of the torment of his passion allowed for the God of possibilities to once again bring order out of chaos. From the darkness of the cross, to the ashes of martyrdom, from scandal, suspicion, and speculation years ago to today, the church has survived and thrived because of imperturbable faith in the phenomenal power of God to speak goodness and holiness into pain, sadness, and misery. For a church that stretches and reaches back into the far edges of history, endurance has been the promise of survival. The growing and changing, the repenting and reawakening of the church over the course of time means that the future, for those who can weather the present darkness, will see the dawning of new ideas and attitudes.

I stood at the ninth station, my fingers intertwined with the cool marble toes of Jesus with no answers and with pain so great it constricted my joy. Yet, beneath the hurt, in the deepest and quietest center of my being a clear and ardent determination bloomed. I will rise from this moment, and I will be present over and over again. Even through agony and the tumbling doubts, I will let my presence speak what I could not form into words. I will endure so that my story endures. I am a Catholic woman, a member of the body of Christ; I have been baptized as priest, prophet, and king. I am not a burden or a nuisance. I am intelligent, capable, and lovable. My God dwells in me and with me just as much as

God is in and with them. I am a Catholic woman, and this is my church.

Love,
Meghan

DEAR MEGHAN,

Your letter confronts us with the problem of abuse without redress. When we find ourselves at the mercy of precisely the people and the institutions from which we have a right to expect defense, that's when we are most likely to collapse under the double strain of the negativity, the disdain, the rejection, the pressure that comes instead. Then what do we do? Ignore it? Quit it? Confront it? What?

The point of what seems to be your unasked question is a distressing one. The fact is that Jesus fell at the hands of both the high priests of the temple and Pilate, the governor of the client territory. By both temple and throne, that is. There was no recourse, no justice to be had, no likely chance of change in either body. Even the local people who had once cheered him on were now jeering him. There was simply no support coming from any direction. The struggle was over. The resistance had been useless. The system had won.

That situation is not only a common one; it is a constant one. It happens everywhere, every day. It is betrayal at its worst.

So the question is not can a woman endure the pain of rejection. Answer: Of course she can. And she has for generations. But the question now is should anyone willingly sustain such abuse rather than resist. And, if so, how?

There are at least three options, of course, in every situation of public conflict of opinions.

First, we can accept reality as the power center now defines it and accept whatever happens to us as a result.

Women, especially women's religious orders, have been in that situation often over the centuries and even in the last decades. In the '60s the canonical legal position was that women religious were subject to the mandates of a local bishop. At least initially, many groups accepted this. But not all. In California, for instance, one group did not accept the bishop's mandate to wear uniform clothing, the medieval habit. When the local bishop denounced them for it publicly, they renounced the canonical standing that identified them as a religious order and to this day function as a lay community outside of diocesan direction.

You can resist, in other words, as long as you realize the consequences and are willing to bear them.

Second, we can resist an order and try to work through the differences to the point of mutual understanding.

Many groups of women religious did that too. They went back and forth from the United States to Rome year after year hoping that enough discussion with members of the Curia would eventually resolve what Rome considered unacceptable about their Renewal Constitutions. In our case, they wanted us to insert Marian theology in a Benedictine Constitution. Finally, we wrote a paragraph about the Marian Antiphons we sing at Vespers during the year, and they approved the Constitutions that said nothing at all about Marian spirituality being fundamental to the Benedictine charism. Which, of course, it is not.

That kind of relentless review of an already incorrect interpretation takes patience, takes commitment, takes the strength to claim who I am and insist on remaining who I am. It is a leveling of rights and responsibilities on both sides and can make mutuality possible.

Or, third, we can ignore the question entirely and go on without either approval or public identification with the authority in question. It puts a group in limbo, but if neither side issues an ultimatum, it also begins the building of a new world, hoping that the old world will eventually catch up with us—as Vatican II did by recognizing the Christianity of non-Catholic Christians over four hundred years later, though still withholding a common Eucharist.

In your letter, you make an explicit claim to enduring institutional abuse—as Jesus did—which is, however, too often taken for granted from women. You stand in a strong tradition. The only question left is how you intend to do that so that the world, the church, and women, too, may all grow to the fullness of themselves over time.

Suffering in silence when the suffering is patently unjust may only serve to increase pain for everyone else as well. On the other hand, to continue to name the evil, to continue to call for justice, to refuse to be silent, can only encourage others to do the same. Then, someday, the Voices of Justice will rise together, remember, and drive the changes we need.

With support always,

Joan

Dear Joan,

We were rinsing dishes in the *pila* when my Salvadoran mother uttered that she had a *corazón destrozada*, a destroyed heart. We were on that remote-yet-familiar Salvadoran hillside nestled outside the capital on a hot March day. I made the short trip from California to cry and mourn and be with my dear Salvadoran family, whose world had been turned upside down through death—early and violent deaths. No wonder Deysi described herself as having a *corazón destrozada*.

These haunting words shattered the superficial and empty platitude of being "OK," the short response so often uttered when unacknowledged grief hangs thick in the air. An ongoing relationship with my *madre salvadoreña* over the past seven years holds me accountable to the weight of grief, the possibility of joy amid the loss, and the lived meaning of accompaniment and mutuality.

We first met in January 2011, when I was an eager, sophomoric sophomore, a *gringa* enrolled in an alternative study abroad semester, the Casa de la Solidaridad program. The program emphasized accompaniment, spirituality, immersion, and community, with the Salvadoran reality as the primary locus of learning. Two days a week, students spent time walking with and learning alongside Salvadorans—and it was there, in that remote *cantón*, where my heart was broken open in that peculiar paradox of grief and joy. Grief and anguish at the crushing poverty and atrocious civil war and complicity of the United States government; unbelievable joy at the resilient laughter of children; and relentless sharing of communion in the form of tortillas.

Back at the *pila*, Deysi described how her exterior may show strength, but she felt the depths of her pain, a destroyed heart; after all, she had to bury her beloved son and husband in the span of eighteen months. As soon as I walked into their home this time around, the tears began. It felt as if we really needed to lean on each other. We ate watermelon, talked, made tortillas, and settled into a familiar rhythm—though we all knew there were two familiar faces missing from this reunion.

The gut check felt particularly acute that March morning as I attempted to hold the pain of her losses with that of my own.

When I was twenty-one, my family buried my father, his body ravaged with cancer. It was a good death; I was in right relationship with him, and we were all gathered around him when he died.

My Salvadoran mother invited me to consider, in her humble, maternal way, how to sit with a destroyed heart and how to be courageous enough to be blessed, broken, and shared, drawing strength from community in order to be communion for others.

And so we went on, washing dishes, allowing the tears to fall, the heavy absence of loved ones deeply felt. And we *sigue adelante*, we keep walking. How can we invite others to be vulnerable? How do we accompany others in the midst of grief and pain?

In love and vulnerability,
Lisa

Dear Lisa,

I think your questions get to the core of people's desire to be helpful, loving, and effectual in working with those whose lives have been interrupted by tragedy. At the same time, you open some areas of discomfort too. For instance, how much "understanding" is too much understanding? When what the wounded need is emotional recovery and resurrection of spirit, plying them with stories of pain—

our own or someone else's—is useless, if not wearying. Of course, it's necessary to understand devastation and depression, but understanding is not a substitute for support. For instance, your question "How can we invite others to be vulnerable?" is a delicate one if you mean, "What can I do to help people open up their hearts," and allow them to tell you their fears and sense of loss without cutting them off, changing the subject, or starting to tell your own stories? Remember always that loss and shock, trauma and fear, can be as numbing as they are emotionally consuming. The truth is that a person in the midst of life-changing trauma may talk sparingly, if at all. Which means that the rest of us must listen carefully for the hints of fear or pain we can help them to express.

Then when you are about to tell your own stories, stop and listen some more. Most of all, don't impose on someone else what you assume they should be feeling. Or thinking. Or doing right now.

We do not, in other words, "invite" people to be vulnerable by intruding on the private space they need or by insisting that they talk to us. That kind of ministry is more about the needs of the minister than it is sensitivity to the needs of the needy.

What's important is that we allow people to express their feelings. It's vital that we give the victim of shock, loss, fear, powerlessness a chance to be honest themselves rather than tell them "Don't cry," or, "It will be all right," or "Be brave," or, alternatively, "You just need a good cry." Instead, go where they lead you rather than try to fit them into your preferred issues or style of dealing with pain.

Otherwise, ministry becomes an exercise in the minister's image making, not empathy. To give real spiritual help, remember the death of Jesus' friend Lazarus and the fact that the Scripture says, "And Jesus wept." Cried. Jesus. Cried.

The lesson is obvious. Pain is acceptable, and we do not help a person recover by denying them the right to express it. Feelings of despair are normal and cannot be talked away or discounted or drowned out by the telling of our own personal stories. What can give a person more right to be allowed to grieve than the complete eruption of their entire life? What the person in pain needs is the right to own the pain, the anger, the frustration, the cry for support. They do not need gushing news about how we think "it will be all right." Of course, it will be all right. But what they need in the here and now is the opportunity for the pain to be heard and acknowledged. Not staunched. Not suppressed. Just heard and received.

It's essential, too, that what we say is meaningful, not simply chatter meant to cover up the embarrassment of the pain. Rather than attempt to smother the pain with empty words or, worse, directions, it's important that we do two things.

First, we must help a person in pain to create a spiritual image they can hang on to and own. Yes, Jesus suffered, too, but what cannot be forgotten is that Jesus raised wounded people from the depths of despondency then and goes on doing the same for us now. The blind beggar, the woman "who had not stood upright for eighteen years," the grieving women at the empty tomb who all found new hope in Jesus remind us, remote as new life may now seem in the midst of deadening pain, that the Christian message is clear: hope lives.

Second, we must do the little things for people that are necessary at the time: contact friends, define arrangements, get meals, clean the house, sit by, and wait—for signs of need or cries for help. It's the kinds of thing you refer to in your letter as you do the dishes and get a little lunch. It is the call to do "whatever" so that the wounded can, instead, cry.

Those are the ways we "accompany" people, meaning, do what we can to help them move through this moment to the next. We must realize, too, that the way through grief, pain, and shock can be a very long journey. It's not resolved overnight. Two years after my best friend died, other friends reminded me that I was not alone. They sent text messages. They made phone calls to say that they were aware of how long pain lingers beneath the surface of the soul. They took me places and did things with me I would never have done alone. And doing that they replaced the images that can go on haunting today with yesterday for a long, long time.

People feel truly "accompanied" when they have proof—actual proof—that they are not alone on this long road to new life.

The "ministry" of Jesus is more than just dropping in to repeat standard clichés. It is about long-term presence that doesn't overpower a person. It makes the move to tomorrow smoother for them than it would be if they had to do it alone.

That's the ministry people need at the time of pain. That's the empathy we must develop in ourselves. We need to learn that compassion is not about saying the right things at the right time; that's sympathy. Empathy is about feeling the pain of the other. It means that we do for another what no funeral script or liturgy can supply but which the suffering cannot do without some help. That is the real Jesus moment, the moment of honesty and love and resurrection to new life.

The authentic part of your own ministry is that you are asking yourself what accompaniment is really all about rather than assuming that a degree in ministry automatically qualifies anyone to be an authentic part of another person's grief and loss.

You are asking specific questions about what it means to minister to the vulnerable. Your letter indicates that you realize that effective "accompaniment" of the poor, the wounded, the outcasts, the broken will be more than momentary. Accompaniment must be emotionally honest—meaning genuinely caring, seriously listening, and deeply committed to making the present bearable and the future conceivable for those for whom today feels impossible, physically, emotionally, or both.

Finally, accompaniment—the bridge between uncertainty and a new normalcy—requires patience and presence. Those who choose to accompany another through the deep, dark parts of life must learn to allow the wounded themselves to lead the way. What the wounded need to know is that someone is standing by, bearing the heat of the day with them, until they have the personal strength to take on a new life of their own. However long it takes.

With encouragement and care,
Joan

Dear Joan,

I never thought that I would pursue my faith or obtain a ministerial degree. My twelve-year-old self would be shocked that my passion and truth revolve around empowering women's voices, especially in the church. With the power of mercy, however, I should not be too surprised. Mercy led me to dedicating my life to ministry. It motivated me to transcend canonical confines and face my personal woundedness.

When I was twelve, my father unexpectedly left my family. His actions and behavior led my mother to receive full custody of my twin sister and me. With her duty to raise two children, my mother did her best to take us to church. However, the annulment process seemed to wound her more. I vividly remember joining the Eucharistic procession as my mother cried in her pew. It was painful to witness how she felt unworthy to participate in and receive communion. Attending church became a constant reminder of the brokenness of our family. Each Sunday became harder and harder to attend until we stopped going altogether.

My father's neglect impacted my faith. In my adolescence, I struggled to pray to a Father when my own was associated with abandonment. I strongly felt that God abandoned me. I gave power to my biological father. Simultaneously, I gave power to the Divine Masculine as you described in your compilation of writings. My God was a judge, warrior, lawgiver, and perfectionist. My God was distant and unemotional. I did not like "Him." I craved and needed the Divine Feminine but did not have a conscious awareness of God as mother. Almost a decade after my parents' divorce, wisdom figures illuminated God's femininity for me. This was a catalyst to my faith and vocation.

I contemplate how others with a similar experience have been affected, where divorce seems to imply failure. I, personally, do not see failure in many situations but rather strength and courage in those who survive it. I strongly feel that we, as a church, need to heal the wounds of the people who have distanced themselves from God through their hardships.

Joan, the church needs to be a beacon of hope and comfort. How can the church reach out to people who have been wounded by an institution whose practices can at times isolate people like my mother? The church needs to tap into its network of women wisdom figures who offer compassion and love to the wounded.

Specifically, there is a need for healthier dialogue within the Catholic Church between those who have experienced divorce and those who have not. My mother persevered through her pain, yet her implied failure made her think she was unworthy to receive the Eucharist. Her sense of "unworthiness" had an impact on me as a woman.

My worthiness was revolutionized when I began to understand that God is not the culprit of my pain. You, Joan, helped me to articulate that.

Peace,
Liz

DEAR LIZ,

Your very honest and very painful letter reflects a far larger proportion of the church than most of us would like to admit, I'm afraid. What the church has done to women and how the church images God to women—both issues so different for women than for men—has left permanent scars on the souls of far too many women. Some have left their religions of origin hoping to find more holiness in other traditions. Just as many have abandoned all religion everywhere in despair of ever finding a God that might be God-like with women. The mainstream, of course, accepted, and taught their daughters to accept as well, that a woman's role in the church was to submit to men, to be subject to male theology, male rules, and male dominance as some sort of punishment for being female in the first place. It was all, they argued, "a woman's place."

Just to see those words in print is enough to feel the implications of them, the pain of them, just as your mother did. According to male interpretations of the Scriptures, childbirth itself was a punishment for being born a woman. Women, "bone of my bone, flesh of my flesh"—somebody made of the same substance as men themselves—were, men decided, emotionally unsound, intellectually incompetent, fundamentally irrational, and sexually dangerous to men who, apparently, could not curb their passions in the presence of a woman.

So women were cloistered, for all intents and purposes, in both the home and the streets, as well as the convents, while men had free rein. Women were denied civil rights even in democratic societies like our own where as recently as fifty years ago, in your grandmother's time, women could not apply for a loan without her husband's permission, sign contracts or promissory notes, get jobs, join public clubs, or negotiate sales, even of her own property, without male authorization.

It's so easy to argue now that "life was just like that—

back then." Or that it happened to women everywhere, so it wasn't just the church that did it. Yet the fact is that it was the God-talk of the churches that maintained it as well as taught it. Wouldn't a woman have the right to think that the church that finally ceased to preach slavery might have led the empowerment and liberation of women too? Except that the control of women served men entirely and everywhere.

Worse yet, these sins done in the name of "women's place" in life are still commonplace around the globe, not in Catholicism only, but in any religion that is male-dominated, as men say it must be. How many sermons have you ever heard about this sin of the church from the pulpit on either Mother's Day or Father's Day?

Indeed, the sin remains. The male image of God remains. The lack of the Divine Feminine remains, a stain on our churches, an affront to Mary of Nazareth and all the women of the church everywhere.

Indeed, your mercy and honesty and strength and hope are needed, Liz, until every woman everywhere is raised to the fullness of her humanity. But that will not happen without the courage of women themselves—women like you, Liz—who speak up and call the church, directly and honestly, to account, demanding change.

With care and courage,
Joan

on standing up to the patriarchy

HERE'S HOW WE KNOW THAT PATRIARCHY IS NOT OVER: Nobody talks about it in past tense.

Better yet, sit and watch television cameras pan the parliaments of the world, the synods of the churches. That's patriarchy. That's where the decisions come from, the rulers are named, the ideas are confirmed, and the population is male. Oh, there are now a smattering of women in some of those places, of course, as in "add women and stir." Nothing serious.

Worse, what we do have is secular. The state, in fact, does a much better job with the gospel than the church.

The church once said a distant, reluctant, careful yes to altar girls. Then they began immediately to limit the possibilities when it would be allowed—as in as long as there were no boys present. Patriarchy spoke quite openly about who was allowed to read the gospel, for instance, and when. Or measured where women could stand on the altar during a service. One priest I heard of even drew boxes around the altar to make sure that women really "did not cross the line."

Patriarchy's point is clear: Men are in charge. Men give the orders. Men make the rules. Men are preferred to women at all times. Men rule the world, including every woman's world.

To speak truth to a patriarchal world is akin to talking about colors to people who are blind or regional accents to people who are deaf or running marathons to people who are crippled. Many men have no experience of being "other" *in terms of gender.* Until, of course, a woman calls them to include in their pantheon of possibilities what it is to be without a voice, without power, without the experience of inclusion. What men have they have by law; and in the church, according to them, it is by virtue of the will of God that they rule the world.

To pierce that kind of exclusiveness takes courage. Takes endurance. Takes persistence. Most of all, it takes refusing to accept the kind of sweet manipulation women were taught to affect in order to get what they needed from the men who had the power to keep it from them. To confront the patriarchy in every woman's life too often comes out of desperation. Then, things get to be so bad that taking it any longer is more impossible than being divorced, derided, or threatened with the verdict of madness.

Dear Joan,

My heart raced like a metronome gone haywire the first time I took a stand.

Most mornings I join a monastic community for Morning Prayer. Reading Scripture is a normal part of the ritual. This particular morning started out as any other. We made the sign of the cross and asked God to come to our assistance. We chanted a few psalms. Then the words of Peter the Apostle boomed through the church: "Women are the weaker sex."

I froze. Did such an insult really just enter this sacred space?

When the reader finished the passage, he bowed to the altar and took his seat. A period of silence began—and I knew I had to make a decision. I spent most of my life self-conscious about my body's location. At a gangly six-feet tall, I tend to draw unwanted attention walking down the street. But the questions of place run deeper. Am I wanted around this table? Have I overstayed my welcome? Do I belong here? These questions became part of the rhythm of my life, ticking away at my confidence and jamming me into the least obtrusive position. In this case, least obtrusive meant staying seated in the choir stalls.

But I could not *not* move. I needed to stand up.

Joan, you told me language matters. You said language can render people invisible. I knew if I stayed seated, my body would send the message that I was comfortable enough with the words just proclaimed. The prayer would go on. I would sing the Canticle of Zechariah, ask God to hear our prayer, and recite the Our Father as if Peter's words were acceptable—or, worse, true.

But I have a different truth to tell.

I believe all people are created in the image of God and deserve to be treated as such. I reject the notion that women are the "weaker sex." I long for freedom for females everywhere, freedom to be who we are called to be and to do what we are called to do. In the moment of silence at Morning Prayer, I knew the ramifications of staying seated and allowing Peter's words to be the unopposed truth were far more harmful than any feeling of self-consciousness that may arise from stepping out of place.

So with hands shaking and a metronome heart racing, I closed the prayer book, folded up my seat, and walked alone to the door. I went to my office and, with a warm cup of coffee in hand, finished Morning Prayer with a new Scripture passage: "You are the salt of the earth. You are the light of the world. Let your light shine before others..."

It turns out others were bothered by the 1 Peter passage. The experience prompted conversations on patriarchy, prayer, and social position in the days that followed. I'm hopeful that, together, praying communities can stand up for a better, more inclusive beat. Scripture is filled with masculine language and troubling statements about women. How might we handle this in parishes?

Peace,
Jessie

Dear Jessie,

Nothing will ever replace the value of the maturation process your letter describes. The first truth is that women everywhere are born into patriarchal systems that suppress their development, limit their opportunities, and sacrifice their abilities, ideas, insights, and talents to the worship of god-the-mighty-male. No matter how heretical that very notion can possibly be.

But the next truth is that in this era, education and sister-hood is awakening women to the genuine sinfulness of any system that raises itself to power on the backs of the pow-erless. The ability to keep women ignorant, enchained, and unaware of their own power and the gift of their very exis-tence is over now. We are growing up.

At the moment of our own enlightenment, conscious-ness becomes the Holy Grail to which we commit ourselves for women everywhere. Consciousness commits. Once aware of the power and meaning of our own creation, there is no going back to the acceptance of inequality.

Which is where this letter touches the issue that is at the cutting edge of male-female equality. When we become con-scious of the language that creates the reality around us, we can begin to hope for real change. As you did, Jessie, when you actually heard the sexism that holds the gospel at bay.

"Women are the weaker sex," the writers quote Peter as saying. Various commentators interpret the meaning dif-ferently—as conservative, as cultural, as metaphorical, as feminist. But frankly, that's not the problem. The problem is the language itself and what it means to many in our own day and age. It is the kind of thing that translators deal with daily—and routinely solve with synonyms or interpola-tions. The problem is that the church of our age doesn't even see a need to deal with it at all.

As a result, women are left out of the very pronouns of the church, the gospel, the homilies of the age. We say "he" when we say we mean both men AND women. But every day that kind of language is less and less amenable to personal translation. If you think the words really mean both men and women, then say so.

Language is the weapon the church uses against women—and says it doesn't really mean anything and we should all just ignore it. But since it doesn't mean anything let's take "Jesus came to save all men"—which we've been saying for almost two thousand years, whatever it really meant—and, since they say it doesn't mean anything, from now on say, "Jesus came to save all women." And tell them they should "just ignore it." (After all, at least the word "women" includes the word "men"—which is better than we're doing right now.)

But we know what men—especially male clerics, theologians, hierarchy—would say about using "she" and "woman" to mean everyone. Which of course tells us all we need to know about what it means for them to continue using "man" and "he" exclusively.

The fact is that language makes things visible, gives them importance, shapes our thoughts by making conscious what we see, draws our attention to things, affects our consciousness of others, of ourselves. When men hear only about male images at prayer the effects are obvious. When God is always male, males find it easy to believe that they are Gods too. When women are subsumed by "they," or "he," or "men"—always, always, always—they never become "her," "she," and "women" let alone part of the Divine Feminine.

Or to put it another way: Every day of my life in their church, I never, ever see myself in their church.

How might we handle this? Easily. Turn the sentences into what they are meant to be about: men and women. Equally.

And so that that might happen, Jessie, remember, "You are the salt of the earth. You are the light of the world." And for all our sakes, "Let your light shine before *others*..."

With support and care,
Joan

Dear Joan,

One of my favorite Scripture passages is the story in 1 Kings when God appears to Elijah on Mount Horeb—not in the great and powerful wind that shattered rocks, not in the rumbling earthquake or the raging fire, but in a gentle, quiet whisper.

Introvert that I am, I can relate to God's decision to speak through a gentle whisper. When it comes to speaking my truth and standing up to the patriarchy, that's the path I take. I don't speak in front of crowds, or organize a community of protesters, or create a sizable presence on social media. I ask quiet questions.

The first time I realized the fierceness of quiet questions was when I became acquainted with a new pastor at the parish where I work as the director of faith formation. For the first several months of our working relationship, he bore a pained expression when I asked to meet with him, sighed if I had too many questions, and groaned if I had more than one or two items to discuss with him. Though I both resented and felt intimidated by his behavior, I tolerated it for a variety of reasons. He's new and overwhelmed, I told myself. He has so much on his plate and meeting with me is just one more thing. He acts this way because he's not happy with my work. This is my fault.

These thoughts cycled through my mind on repeat until one day when I grew so frustrated that I chose to hit the pause button on the cycle. Instead of accepting the explanations I was given, I began to ask myself some questions: Am I doing my best to serve this parish where we both minister? Am I entitled to his input and advice? Am I worthy of his time?

As I answered yes to each of these questions, further questions emerged: What's going on here? Why am I allowing myself to be treated in a way that I would never accept from a friend, parent, my husband, or a different co-worker? Can I speak up to my priest? Can I confront the patriarchy as it is revealing itself in my neck of the woods?

From these questions, another one bubbled up, and this one I spoke aloud.

"Is everything all right?" I asked my priest as he sighed loudly during a check-in meeting I had scheduled.

"Oh, yes, it's fine," he quickly replied.

"You're sighing; you seem either bored or upset. Are you?" I pushed on.

As I waited for his reply to my quiet but direct question, he grew momentarily flustered, and then, like flipping a switch, his countenance changed. He sat up straighter and gave me his full attention. We went on to have a more fruitful conversation about the programs I was working on than we ever had before. We both smiled as we left the meeting.

Looking back, I see that this short conversation, of which my question was the pivotal point, transformed our working relationship. From my perspective, he began to see me as a peer rather than a subordinate. I grew more comfortable speaking openly and freely. Deeper mutual respect was born of my courage to confront his behavior and, more important, my decision to stop passively accepting the silent but insidious rules of the patriarchy, the rules that say "his time is the most valuable; his behavior, because it's understandable, is acceptable; his work is the only important work."

A change happened in both of us during that meeting, a change that has led to greater abundance in our individual lives, our working relationship, and our parish, which benefits from collaborative leadership. Standing up to the patriarchy is good for the life of the church.

Sincerely,
Teresa

Dear Teresa,

In the interests of clarity, let's you and me also be direct and honest: If you think that the question you asked the new priest-pastor was "quiet," you either don't know a lot about power or you prefer to pretend you have none. Volume is not the way to measure a powerful question. A powerful statement is a statement that is honest, direct, and important to the people and the situation. Power has to do with being honest, speaking directly, having a clear purpose. You rang all three bells in the conversation you describe for us.

First, you were secretly depressed at the way the team conversations with the new pastor had been going, and you were honest about it to yourself. At least as far as you were concerned, something was missing in the work you were doing for the parish. He was barely paying attention to your reports and requests for feedback. You knew it and he knew it too.

Second, you unmasked the ghost in the room by naming it out loud: "Are you bored or upset?" is not one of those remarks that have no pertinent emotional value. Like, "Cold day, isn't it? Shall I turn up the thermostat?" To ask some- one if they are "bored" or "upset" by your presence is to insist on some face-to-face analysis. Which, incidentally, takes a great deal of courage.

And third, your honesty and directness were essential to the work at hand, to the relationship, to the success of the ministry itself. There are three kinds of power: *Power over*, *power with*, and *power for*. *Power over* people enables one person to control the others. *Power with* others is collaborative. Power used for the sake of the good of others is *power for*. It was the kind of power that would make your parish itself stronger for which you risked the questions.

Finally, not only was the question itself "quiet," as in civil, but it was also not accusatory. Maybe the priest had himself not felt invited into the conversation. The grace was that someone enabled the conversation to be opened, to be resolved. Then, when someone asked the right question in the right way, you could now, you both knew, be honest with one another. Now that is not force—which is violent on every possible level, no matter how softly spoken. But it is powerful because it requires us to face ourselves and to allow others to face us too.

The reason patriarchy works—in churches, in marriages, in occupational positions— is because people encourage it to exist, or allow it to, or prefer to complain about it rather than to confront it. Women, most or all, are deterred from confronting it. After all, the power imbalance has been written into the theology of the church! Self-editing in women too—the need to be thought of as "nice," as in not "aggressive"—often makes it impossible for women "to push on," to persist, as you did. Or, worse, the threat of losing the position itself as a result of being honest about it can weigh heavily in the favor of "authority" and so allow patriarchy to grow like mold on the walls of our institutions.

But for those who believe that the risk is worth it, as you did, great good can occur not only for the patriarchs of the world but for people at large. After conversations like this, the equality model begins to seep into the population itself. Silently, usually, but always effectively.

In the church, when it is done persistently, honestly, as you did, not to upend a ministry but to balance it, the entire parish begins to be a real community. When the people of the church realize that they are 99% of the church itself, then priesthood, the other 1%, will become a ministry of brotherhood, not lordship, and both the people and the priest will find themselves in it—together.

For right now, the point is this: Like Elijah, don't confuse force and power. Force is meant to control, to diminish the other. The right use of power enables people to be both honest and strong without being destructive.

With courage,

Joan

Dear Joan,

"How are we going to sing a new church into being? And if we don't do it, who will?"

I offered these questions on the first day of new student orientation at my graduate school. Each year, two returning students are asked to prepare and preside over a Liturgy of the Word for the new students. This year, a Jesuit scholastic friend and I co-presided. I offered the reflection after the gospel.

It was one of the most difficult reflections I have given. Less than two weeks before, the Pennsylvania grand jury report had been released, detailing the heinous crimes committed by hundreds of priests and the subsequent and equally despicable episcopal cover-up. How do you preach to students who are committing to study and ministry within the Catholic Church when that same church seems to be falling apart in front of them? How do we move from a place where power is abused and where silence is the solution to a place of hope for the future?

Afterward, students and faculty filed past me as they headed to lunch. Many students shook my hand, thanking me for my words.

One new student told me she had never heard a woman preach before, something she previously thought not possible.

Another student said my words moved him to tears.

Some professors embraced me, gently thanking me with an extra pat on the back.

Others asked me to send them a copy of the reflection so that they could pray with it in the coming weeks.

What struck me most was one professor who hung back slightly, not saying anything, instead catching my gaze and nodding her head, the moisture in her eyes apparent.

Despite the clear impact of my words, I would rather not be in the pulpit in the first place. I'd rather cantor or lead children's choir or simply be a part of the congregation. However, sometimes standing up to the patriarchy requires leaving our comfort zones. In preaching, I'm forced to take my questions to heart. How can we empower others to do the same? How can we enable other women to preach? How can we encourage lay leadership in our own parishes and dioceses?

Unlike many women in the church, I am in a position to preach in a liturgical setting. By doing so, I help to normalize the role of women as vessels of the word of God. Being a lay woman at the pulpit in the Catholic Church is a revolutionary act. It touches the congregation in a different way. And, after hearing countless homilies from ordained men all their lives, how could it not be impactful? God speaks through all our lives, not just the lives of priests and deacons. I've seen you preach with your life, and it has inspired me to preach with both my life and my words, at least until all women can stand at the pulpit with me. I'm not leaving.

With love,
Ellen

Dear Ellen,

The question you ask is one of the central questions of the modern church. It is no longer enough just to sit and wait. Women must organize women to develop their ideas, to risk their discussions, to challenge the anemic status quo, to raise new questions by giving new answers to old questions.

The call now is for women to refuse to be excluded from the male questions and sessions of the church. I remember that years ago—in the '70s—I talked often about holding shadow episcopal conferences and then publishing the women's answers to the major questions of the local church parallel to the documents that came out of episcopal conferences. Then the laity could insert themselves into the discussion, invited or not. For some reason, I never got around to holding those parallel conferences. I regret that. So I am leaving it for you and your generation to do now....

The old warning, "Let not a woman's voice be heard in the church" is a clue to what must be done: Speak. Speak everywhere. About everything. And publish your collected questions and answers. Much like this very book itself.

First, we must begin to think of preaching as "mounting the pulpits of our lives." And how can you do that? Easy: By publishing serious summaries of every event, for instance.

Invite your women friends to give a prayer and a few moments of reflection about the issues or events of the day: at private or personal birthday parties, for instance.

Ask women to speak at family gatherings—at jubilees where they talk about the spirituality of marriage, or at retirement dinners when the work this person has done is being celebrated, or at the baptisms of their nieces, nephews, and grandchildren.

Use celebratory gatherings to mark the new job or the first published paper or the public seminar one of them spoke at, or their admission to institutes or graduate studies or as the first lay pastor of a local church.

Ask women friends to give their reflections on any and all important issues and events of the day.

Give women the opportunity to speak seriously and profoundly about their own spiritual concerns, or public policies, or reflections on policies and politics in the light of the life of Jesus or the teaching of the church. You must speak up, yes, but you must also create every possible platform for other women to speak, to question, to challenge.

Most of all, bring women together to give prepared speeches on the church questions of the time. Refuse to allow questions to be suppressed. One of our most important tasks now is to refuse to allow the questions of the ordination of women, the nature of ordination under any circumstances, the role and place of the female diaconate... to fade away. If women do not keep those questions alive it will take another seventy-five years to legitimate the question itself, let alone begin again a deep and serious consideration of its many possible answers.

Only questions that discomfit either you or them are really worthy of asking. Those must be the homilies we insist on giving, somewhere, somehow: in blogs or letters to the editor, in tweets, in the columns you publish and the books you write. And, of course, at every non-eucharistic service you have, women must speak. At eucharistic services we must insist that women be included as lectors and ministers at the altar and that girls be altar servers. Until we are finally accustomed to seeing women there, how will we ever argue that they are being left out? Men know that this very image is the strongest of them all—which is exactly why they are resisting it with such force, however "legal" it now appears to be.

All the while, remember that none of this is about "winning"—there is no such thing. It is about planting, pruning, nurturing, about mulching and watering, about hoeing and weeding and gathering the reflections, challenges, and questions of women, too, to enable the church to grow from one era to the next. As Paul said of himself when the church was in infancy, "I planted, Apollo watered, but God gave the growth" (1 Corinthians 3:6–9).

The real truth is that "Time changes nothing. People do." Which means that when women themselves take on the mind of the minister, the great ministry of women can come to fullness.

Joan

Dear Joan,

When I think about standing up to the patriarchy, I think about the ways a gentle presence can soften hearts and change systems. I love the saying "gently does it." It reinforces the idea that change can occur when we slow down and listen to the personal stories of people and connect through avenues of empathy and compassion. However, when I think about challenging how women are perceived in the church I find the balance between gentleness and action a struggle. When do I say something, and when do I listen? When do I allow the mystery of God to be discovered through contemplation, and when do I take a stand?

Theologian Susan Smith says the Holy Spirit empowers "humankind to free itself from oppressive structures." As a teacher, I often question: How do I teach this? How do I model it? The religious education classroom in my native Australian schools offers a curriculum that allows students to start questioning what is right and wrong using the guiding model of Jesus and the traditions of the Catholic Church. The curriculum is gentle, self-reflective, and courageously responsive at the same time. Written by both men and women, our curriculum focuses on building relationships between God and people around us. It provides a platform for students to question the status quo. It invites both young people and educators to become gentle, born of wisdom (James 3:17) and active in change.

This year, my school community took on the theme "What would Jesus do?" It is a source of motivation for students to consider what is the right action to take through the lens of Jesus. In a unit about social justice, I asked my Catholic Studies class if they thought Jesus was ever angry. They thought not. "He is perfect," these sixteen-year-old students said. "He cannot get angry."

I challenged them to think bigger. "Isn't part of being Catholic to question the wrongs we see in the world?" The students reconsidered. Then I offered the example of Jesus at the temple. "Is that not a perfect Jesus getting upset?" I questioned. The lesson ended with students realizing that to be like Jesus is to stand up to injustices and not to sit on the sidelines.

This includes standing up to the patriarchy. Being gentle is in no way what makes women and men weak or makes women less motivated for change. It makes us brave. As a teacher I endeavor to be brave and to inspire it. I want the students I teach to question the world and their faith in the search to make the world a better place for both women and men.

Yours in being brave,
Eliza

Dear Eliza,

Like you, I prefer the soft and gentle way through life. But when I was a young sister, I found myself confronted by some terrible truths.

A president of the United States had lied to the American people in order to justify the invasion of Vietnam. Young men from mid-America and young people from burning Vietnamese villages were dying in Vietnam for political reasons, not to avenge injustice at all.

African Americans were being kept in a segregated system that denied them civil rights, decent jobs, equal opportunities to expand their lives, and even the right to have lunch at public lunch counters while dogs snarled around their feet.

The church, I learned, had taught that women were weak, irrational, emotional, and inferior to the males of the world. So, despite all scientific data, human experience, and theology to the contrary, like our black brothers and sisters, women were also being kept "in their place." And the church said not a word about any of those things.

I could feel the frustration, the weariness, the tension, the resistance growing within me. Where was all of this going? Why didn't somebody do something about it? When was this feeling going to end? I was angry.

It took a while, but eventually, feeling powerless and very alone socially, I began to realize that I was angry. More than that, I realized that anger was a gift of the Holy Spirit too. Anger, I began to understand, wasn't something to get rid of. Anger was a fuel that fired the engine of change. It was a signal that people—I myself—were beginning to reject whatever racism, sexism, and institutionalized violence held them captive.

Anger, I realized later, was a sign that the human conscience was finally waking up. And these things simply could not be allowed to go on.

It was a moment of great soul-searching. As you say so well, there are questions to answer: What is the line between Holy Anger and passive, blind obedience? How do we know when to listen, when to speak up?

There are two dimensions to anger. First, anger is a Holy Act when its purpose is to transform evil into good. But, second, anger is one thing when it is male, and another thing entirely when it is female. The first thing to remember about anger is that it is genderized. When a man is angry it's called authoritative, justified, justice-seeking. It is a tool they legitimize to control people. When a woman is angry, society says that she is emotional, out of control, irrational. No doubt about it: women, we learn young, are meant to be "gentle"—meaning quiet, unflappable, pacifying in their approach.

So women learn very young to suppress frustration, to say, "Oh, that's alright. Really." when she should be saying, "No!" Or "Never again!" Women are also prone, as a result, to temporize too long with insult and degeneracy, in the hope that the offender, the harasser, the rapist will just quietly go away. Or she finds herself having to defend her civility when the lawyer asks her, "Tell me, Miss Gentility. Did you ever actually say no to my client?"

Clearly, anger is a signal, a protective shield against being overrun by evil and, just as bad, being made powerless by the powerful who have no intention of listening to her needs and her insights and her frustrations and her compassion for the world.

Indeed, the fact that your school curriculum leaves room for the questions, the reflection, the understanding by students that anger has a worthy, an important, and a holy place in a cultivated society is surely among our best teachings. Otherwise the idea that any society can remain highly cultured, deeply civilized, for very long is suspect. But the curriculum must also train those students, especially girls, to speak their anger clearly and definitively. There must be no doubt what a woman wants and why she wants it or that she intends to get it.

Just as important, we must all come to realize that a woman's anger is simply to be respected. It can also be a force for good, for peace, for hope. Healthy anger comes from compassion. Anger itself must "do no harm." It is meant to see the pain of others and not only commiserate with it but set out to transform it into justice.

The purpose of anger is to transform apathy and oppression into resistant anger, into holy action. It is its own answer to the question "When should I speak and when should I be quiet?" It is the bedrock question of modern society.

With courage,

Joan

Dear Joan,

A great privilege and blessing in my life was attending Saint Mary's College for my undergraduate education. This Catholic, all-women's institution located in Notre Dame, Indiana, was founded by the Sisters of the Holy Cross. The charisms of the Sisters illuminate social justice, community, learning, and faith—each creating a strong foundation and catalyst to personal discovery. When I graduated from Saint Mary's College in 2013, I felt invincible, fueled by the fact that all leadership positions at the college are held by women. Perhaps a little naive to the complexities of equality and ominous societal truths, I was empowered to make a difference in both local and global communities.

Years after graduation I decided to pursue a ministerial degree to prepare for work in a patriarchal church. I carried the wisdom of women from Saint Mary's College with me as I entered a male-dominated world. I would not let the new atmosphere deflate my spirit, I thought. My graduate education led me to Nairobi, Kenya, to serve as a hospital chaplain. There I was a member of a small peer group of twelve students, which included a rich and robust mix of cultural, pastoral, and academic experiences. In terms of gender, only three of the twelve students were female. I was the only laywoman among brothers, sisters, and priests. I was also the only American in a class of mostly Kenyans. It was an interesting juxtaposition to be aware of my privilege as an American while representing the minority as a laywoman. Toward the end of my immersion experience, an ordained peer challenged me. He said, "Your faith is not as strong as the rest of us because you have not taken vows." Shocked by his words, I asked him to repeat himself, as if I had misheard his original statement. After clarifying that I had indeed heard him correctly, I felt my blood pressure rise and my face redden as I defended my place in the class and the church. I also felt compelled to defend my relationship with God as if his words triggered insecurity that I was "less than" because I had not taken vows.

I despised how this encounter made me feel. I felt disturbed with myself when his words triggered insecurities. I reflected on a broader problem: how both society and church can make women feel inferior. In the midst of that reflection, I felt a new responsibility to engage in dialogue about the truth of my vocation as a laywoman, a vocation that equally contributes to the common good. My peers and I have recognized an inherent loneliness that accompanies this vocation. Priests, brothers, and sisters find community and support in their congregations. Meanwhile, I am judged by many in my generation who do not see vitality in faith or who passively suggest, "Why don't you just become a nun already?" I have had to knit together my own tribe and suppress my frustration when friends and family do not fully understand my pursuit of faith as a laywoman.

Joan, on this topic, I have turned to your words often. You said, "The moment a woman comes home to herself, the moment she knows that she has become a person of influence, an artist of her life, a sculptor of her universe, a person with rights and responsibilities who is respected and recognized, the resurrection of the world begins."

I am determined to contribute to that resurrection as a laywoman. How are we each called to pursue our faith in our unique vocations?

Peace,
Liz

Dear Liz,

If there is anything in the decretals of the church that remains unfinished, it is surely the theology of vocation. To try to think your way through "ministry" in the Catholic Church is itself a foreign language. Who can really interpret it? Unless you understand the patriarchal system itself and the ladders it devises to demonstrate itself, the whole system is a maze. Only one element of it is clear: In this system everywhere, clerical men dominate laymen and all women. And theirs, of course, is the "highest" vocation. Highest meaning what? Closest to God, more important than its church counterparts, or most likely to be sanctifying?

Priesthood is the "highest" of vocations, they tell us. But why that is or how it can be that men can make so many varieties of it for men but not for women is anybody's guess. Nor how it is that only males can enter into the fullness of ministry on the basis of maleness alone defies the very theology of baptism.

Priesthood, we're told, is also celibate in the Roman Catholic rite—except that in seven of the eight major rites of the church it is not. Married priests abound in every ethnic dimension of the church except the Roman rite. Then, in some other rites, only bishops must be celibate, and priests may be married before ordination but not after. This "highest" of all vocations is clearly a movable feast where being the best is concerned.

The second of the vocations, they told us, was "the religious life," communal lifestyles approved by the church but differing in spiritual disciplines, public and private works, and male, female, or mixed in membership. "Religious"—those who belonged to canonical communities and vowed to commit themselves to this kind of celibate life forever—were "high" vocations, whatever that meant, but not as high a vocation as priests. Except that male communities could also be priests, which left the orders of brothers, who were never ordained, as only "religious" and so not so "high" either.

And then there was a third vocation, they said. But they told us nothing about it. Nothing at all. Except that these were unmarried "laypeople who stayed single"—unmarried—all their lives. No mention of vows. No mention of purpose. No mention of spiritual disciplines. No mention of whether they were a "high" vocation or not. No mention.

Married couples, the only ones of all the types, except priests, of course, that had a sacrament, were not in the list at all. Go figure.

This dismissal of the lay vocation in the world was an incalculable, but obvious, loss to the church and to the world. And still is. Not until the Decree on the Laity at Vatican II, which may well turn out to be one of its most momentous achievements, had anyone even begun to define the role and place of the committed layperson on the real impact of the church on the world.

This is what all of you are doing now. Still overlooked. Still too often ignored. And yet, with the priesthood smaller by the day and religious life still largely institutionally defined and, as always, the small portion of religious vocations, you are the people taking the church to the center of the church, to the center of the world.

It may well be the lay vocation that saves the church this time and—if the drain of young and middle-aged Catholics from active membership in the church is any omen—something better will rise to give it new life; if not, the dynamism of the tradition as we have known it may disappear before our very eyes. Just when a classist and divided country needs it most.

With commitment,
Joan

Dear Joan,

It was a Sunday evening and I was sitting on my living room floor with the debris of a research project surrounding me. My computer was precariously balanced on my knee, when a new email from my professor flashed across the screen. The words danced into my vision.

Pointless. Useless. Worthless.

I had conceived of and dismissed these words with difficulty, before. Now, they appeared in an email to me. About me. They fell off the screen and into my lap with a thud that reverberated throughout my heart and soul.

In the span of four months I had become profoundly deaf. It was sudden. It was unexpected. It was catastrophic. My life as a graduate theology student wavered with uncertainty. In the months since my illness took my hearing, I was advised to quit more times than I was encouraged to continue. Professors and seminarians alike bemoaned any changes to the status quo that provided some sort of accessibility. My presence at the seminary became a target for bad one-liners and disparaging remarks. Like you prophetically warn in *Heart of Flesh*, my soul had been sold for the sake of the system. Not only was my presence not tolerated, it was now, as the email demonstrated, actively opposed. Accommodations in the classroom were denied and removed at the whim of professors who found a (relatively) smart, deaf woman at a Catholic seminary a threat.

Yet I had remained quiet, stalled in a struggle of wanting to keep the peace and wanting justice for myself. I endured the torment of these men, and women, but inside, their words stripped my soul of confidence, drive, and happiness. I had never stood up to the patriarchy before, and I'm not sure I would have ever even acknowledged the patriarchy existing. But the words of that email became a catalyst; they demanded a response. If I didn't fight for my own place in the system, I was buying that place for other women at the expense of my own soul.

And so, on that Sunday night, I made the decision to reject those words written about me. In radical and peaceful disobedience, I showed up to class the next day armed with a new-found determination to persevere in my dream of studying theology. Every class attended, every night spent in the library, every page typed, every "A" earned was a step forward against a system built by and for men. My continued presence and success in the classroom is my way of standing up to the patriarchy, of taking a stand against those men who would rather I be quiet, invisible, submissive. But Joan, as I'm sure you know, this path of determination is lonely. The more I stand up for myself, the more people seem to sit down and back away. How have you navigated a world in which you are not welcome? Where do you find the courage to walk forward, often alone, and proclaim your truth to all those who have stood in your way? When I stand on the stage holding my diploma, I stand with your example in front of me and behind me. I will stand up and proclaim to all of those who stood in my way that I am not pointless, useless, or worthless.

Love,
Meghan

DEAR MEGHAN,

Your letter paints a searing picture of the classism that sexism spawns and so, too, the continuing situation of every woman in the church. Only, your situation is more pointed, in some ways more honest, certainly more hurtful than most. It is bullying at worst.

Ever since Vatican II allowed women to study theology with men—a situation never before permitted until John Paul II's 1979 apostolic constitution *Sapientia Christiana* opened institutions granting ecclesiastical degrees to all. Whether clergy or lay, those were admitted who met the academic prerequisites and could legally testify to leading a moral life. Nevertheless, efforts to discourage women from even attempting to matriculate have been common. Making women students feel uncomfortable, unwanted, unseen has been one of the most favorite responses of them all. And you, Meghan, clearly, got the full treatment.

I myself never tried to join the ranks of theology students on Catholic campuses of any size or distinction. I had done my graduate work at a great university where there were no intellectual fences designed to protect parochial ideas from greater scrutiny.

I did, however, go to church conferences of all ilk where the same tactics were applied. Little things did it best, like saying, "Good morning, Father," to a priest in the corridor who cast his eyes to the floor and did not so much as nod in recognition.

Being blocked out of the coffee table during intermissions was effective too.

Having community dining rooms closed in our faces at lunchtime so the women participants would have to go out to buy lunch rather than get it with the cost of admission was commonplace too. As if the presence of women at a lunch table would upset the "brotherly love" of the group.

Indeed, it was one rejection, one snub after another. It was isolating. It was hurtful. It was divisive. And it was far more theologically rhetorical than any word that could have been said. More, none of us were physically disabled; we were all degreed and perpetually professed religious. But we clearly didn't belong either. So much for Christian ministry, for the priest as the unifier of the parish, the congregation, the church. It made an absolute farce of the gospel in the name of the gospel.

And yet it confirmed in me the need to expose the Christian community as being about one inch deep in its Christianity and miles away from the community of Jesus. With the gospel in one hand and a typewriter in the other, I became committed to the notion that we were being called like Joshua to sound the horn until the walls came crashing down, the last real obstacle to Israel's settlement in the Promised Land.

The situation you describe in this letter not only exposes the kind of sexism, of rejection, that exists at the highest levels of Catholic education but the audacity it takes to extend this kind of exclusiveness even to physical disability. A disability, in fact, that is a memorial to possibility: a deaf woman who asks for nothing but to be allowed to sit in a normal classroom in a normal way. A woman whose brain far exceeds her hearing problem. A woman who will be a model to the rest of us about the normalcy of disability. A woman.

It is impossible not to wonder if a man with a disability would be treated this way in a Catholic school, a Catholic seminary. It also makes us wonder how it is that a Catholic seminary can call itself Catholic at all if this is the operating procedures it supports and models for the rest of the church: its teachings, its witness, its priests.

The abuse and discrimination you detail in this letter are not only unkind, not only immoral, in the fullest meaning of the word, they are illegal. They violate federal and state law. They not only demean you as a woman but also deprive you of your rights as a citizen.

It exposes the link between any kind of difference and the odds against it in the face of privilege, of whiteness, of maleness, of the power balance in society at large. It cries out for change at every level. Such intolerance cannot be tolerated.

The truth is that change of any kind is a process. As one of my professors taught us in Social Psych, remember that eventually everyone has to climb the ladder and step off the high-diving board into the only world available to them now—the new one. But remember, too, that in no society does the whole group dive at once. We all jump into the new water one at a time. It's slow, so slow, always slow.

Welcome to a woman's world, dear Joshua. Remember that it will be the step you take alone that gives the woman behind you the proof that it can be done. Then, finally, all the walls will fall down.

For all our sakes, Meghan, jump.

With pride in all of you,
With love for each.
Joan

CONCLUSION

Dear Reader,

Our decision to share these personal and at times painful stories of sisterhood, speaking truth, and standing up to the patriarchy took discernment. We are well-educated women who know the risks of speaking out against the status quo. We also know the risks of staying quiet and the kind of darkness that looms over life in the shadows. We discerned to share our stories publicly because the God we've come to know in our prayer, study, and work—the God who created all people in the divine image—implores us to live full, authentic lives. Our God is a mysterious one, but this much is clear: we are not called to be darkness.

God calls us to be light.

In the waters of baptism, the church commissioned us to keep the flame of faith alive in our hearts. How do we take up this light-bearing mission today in a church marred by dark sins of clericalism, abuse, and cover-up? The only way we could take up this mission with any integrity is by shining light on what we know to be true: our God-given experiences. We chose to model the transparency and accountability we long to see in our church by simply being ourselves, our whole selves, and nothing but ourselves. And we hope you will do the same.

Are you in?

Drop us a line at **dearjoan19@gmail.com**. We want to hear from you. Which stories resonate with you? How do our truths compare with your own? What support do you need to shine your brightest? Where is the light leading you? Where is the light of your experience needed the most? Let's keep the conversations going, because:

Your stories matter. Your truths matter. You matter.

With hope,

Jessie

More books from
JOAN CHITTISTER

We Are All One

*Reflections on Unity,
Community and Commitment
to Each Other*

CASEBOUND | 112 PAGES | $14.95
4¾" X 6¼" | 9781627853668

Our Holy Yearning

*Life Lessons for Becoming
Our Truest Selves*

CASEBOUND | 112 PAGES | $12.95
4" X 6" | 9781627850469

The Sacred In-Between

*Spiritual Wisdom for
Life's Every Moment*

CASEBOUND | 112 PAGES | $12.95
4" X 6" | 9781627850018

Aspects of the Heart

The Many Paths to a Good Life

CASEBOUND | 112 PAGES | $12.95
4" X 6" | 9781585958719

Songs of the Heart

Reflections on the Psalms

136 PAGES | $12.95 | 4½" X 6½"
9781627854511

God's Tender Mercy

Reflections on Forgiveness

CASEBOUND | 112 PAGES | $10.95
4" X 6" | 9781585957996

The Breath of the Soul

Reflections on Prayer

144 PAGES | $12.95 | 4" X 6"
9781627854580